Practitioner Series

Springer
London
Berlin
Heidelberg
New York
Hong Kong
Milan
Paris
Tokyo

Published in association with the British Computer Society

Other titles in this series:

Ian Gouge

Shaping the IT Organization – The Impact of Outsourcing and the New Business Model

Springer

Ian Gouge, BA
Leeds, UK

British Library Cataloguing in Publication Data
Gouge, Ian
 Shaping the IT organization : the impact of outsourcing and
 the new business model. – (Practitioner series)
 1. Information technology – Management 2. Electronic data
 processing departments – Contracting out 3. Industrial
 organization 4. Organizational change
 I. Title
 658.4'038
 ISBN 1852337273

Library of Congress Cataloging-in-Publication Data
Gouge, Ian
 Shaping the IT organization : the impact of outsourcing and the new business model / Ian Gouge.
   p. cm. – (Practitioner series)
 ISBN 1-85233-727-3 (alk. paper)
 1. Information technology – Management. 2. Industrial management. 3. Organizational change.
 4. Contracting out. I. Title: Outsourcing and the new business model. II. Title. III. Practitioner
 series (Springer-Verlag)
 HD30.2.G68 2003
 004'.068'7--dc21   2003045587

Practitioner series ISSN 1439-9245
ISBN 1-85233-727-3 Springer-Verlag London Berlin Heidelberg
A member of BertelsmannSpringer Science+Business Media GmbH
http://www.springer.co.uk

Typesetting: by Gray Publishing, Tunbridge Wells, Kent
Printed and bound in the United States of America
34/3830-543210 Printed on acid-free paper SPIN 10910207

Contents

Series Editor's Foreword

This is a book about change, very vital in the current business climate. My students will write that we are living in times of unprecedented change, to which I observe that medieval peasants living in an area of widespread famine probably faced more drastic change in their very survival or not. And change is not always welcomed, as evidenced by the quote given to me by my colleagues during some recent restructuring:

> "We trained hard, but it seemed that every time we were beginning to form up into teams we would be reorganized. I was to learn later in life that we tend to meet any new situation by reorganizing and a wonderful method it can be for creating the illusion of progress, while producing confusion, inefficiency and demoralization."
>
> Caius Petronius, Roman Consul AD66.

The beauty of quoting is that you can hit back. So G.K. Chesterton observed:

> "All conservatism is based upon the idea that if you leave things alone you leave them as they are. But you do not. If you leave a thing alone you leave it to a torrent of change."

An IT professional deals with change as part of his/her profession, so much so that I observe the following paradox:

(1) Change causes problems.
(2) IT practitioners solve problems.
(3) The organization with its problems solved can consider changing itself to gain competitive advantage.
(4) The organization changes.
(5) Go to (1).

So if we are successful, we speed up change and create work, and if unsuccessful, the problem remains to be solved. Jobs for life.

My view of change is that it is all about choice. It's a popular misconception that people like choice. In my experience, many people like the idea of having choice, but find exercising it difficult. So much so, that it is quite common not to make a choice. But not making a choice is itself a choice, and not necessarily the best one.

Ian Gouge's book allows IT professionals and others to think about change/choice in a thoughtful, structured way. It contains the essence of what IT is about in an organization. I recommend all IT practitioners and specialists to read it. As an example of not considering change properly, I offer the successful ERP implementation story I heard a few years ago, where in order to make the new system work, two-thirds of the organization's staff were replaced. Some success!

Ray J Paul

Introduction

Undoubtedly there is something in the human psyche that instinctively instils in the majority of us a desire to live and work within frames of reference and conditions over which we have mastery and control. In childhood these traits manifest themselves in the creation of imaginary worlds over which we can preside in some god-like manner. For boys – and grown men when they revert to being boys again! – the archetypal construction has often been the model railway; for girls perhaps dolls and doll's houses. For many in our new high-tech society these traditional pastimes have been supplanted, with the most common manifestation of 'control play' now clearly resident (for the male of the species at least!) in the computer game. What is the desire to take on the persona of Lara Croft or Sir Alex Ferguson but to satisfy a need to enter into another realm where one can manipulate the 'world' around you to achieve the goals you have been set or have set yourself?

Within the world of work this is perhaps little different. To varying degrees, we each attempt to manage the environment that engages us daily, doing things in our own particular way to exert our individuality on the challenges that we face. For the vast majority attempts to influence their working world will be small-scale and utterly subconscious; for some, however, this is patently not the case. The realm of Information Technology (IT) offers those within it a greater freedom to express themselves – and thereby extend a degree of control over their domain – than many other professions. A Programmer, for example, although working within a defined set of rules, parameters, guidelines and standards, is free to code the program they are working on as they see fit, the proviso being that the final deliverable functions as requested. Indeed, even in its ultimate execution, it is an extension of the world-control theme as the Programmer will have effected a change in making something happen.

At the more senior level of IT management, creative opportunities can most often materialize in the definition of an entire system or – the Holy Grail – in the drafting of an IT strategy. Perhaps here there are tangible parallels with the model railway or doll's house in the need to shape, steer, define and organize. At first blush there may seem little that winning the English Premiership or retrieving artefacts from an Egyptian tomb has in common with the definition of a systems strategy; but just break each of these challenges down into their component parts – goals, targets, phases, projects, assumptions, issues and so forth – and you will find the underlying structures are almost identical.

Having made this statement, I would argue that the most significant undertaking allied with a desire to stamp our own designs on a professional environment is, within the IT space, that of the definition of the IT organization. If there is a tendency when drafting an IT strategy for a fanfare launch followed by a failure to manage, monitor or execute, then this tendency is multiplied many-fold when it comes to the organizing of the most critical element of our IT delivery mechanism, i.e. its people.

As with an IT strategy, senior managers love drawing organization charts. It gives them a chance not only to articulate a vision, but also to impose it upon their world. Perhaps the model railway parallel is illustrative: it is akin to being given an enormous box of track pieces – straights and curves and points – and being told to 'build a layout'. There will be some constraints certainly; perhaps the space within which one has to work, the number of track pieces available, the controllers to hand, and so on. These limitations are mirrored in the IT world: the scope of the function, the types of resource employed, perhaps the numbers of man managers within the team. At the end of the exercise there will be either a layout that successfully facilitates the movement of model trains or an organization that allows one to provision computer systems.

Unfortunately, too many senior IT managers and directors – despite appearances to the contrary – approach the definition of their organizations in a haphazard fashion. The technological and business environment in which we now find ourselves demands a newer and more thorough approach to IT organizational modelling and control. Unfortunately, all too often the structures defined are based on old theory and out-dated experience, and are not moulded to the realities of the world in which we work. To conclude our modelling analogy, it might be akin to deploying clockwork models when sophisticated remote control is the order of the day.

The purpose of this book is to explore how one should go about the shaping of an IT organization in such a way as to ensure effective output from the resource within that structure. This analysis is not focused on the drawing of 'organograms', but rather on precisely understanding the elements and challenges within such a definition. We will explore the IT-specific influences on organizational structure and consider how we can align our resource so as to maximize their contribution to the business community they serve. In doing so I will address a number of key topics:

'Considerations for the IT Organization' and 'What is an Organization?' – What are the issues and key considerations for IT from an organizational perspective, and why is the 'shape' of the organization important? We will look at various generic forms of organization, and unique IT components too. In addition to this, I will explore the notion of the 'organization life cycle' and the impact that this can have within the IT environment.

'Why Change?' – If 'traditional' methods of defining our resourcing structures and models continue to deliver business change and benefit, then why is there a need to consider revising our approach in this area? I will argue that business models and pressures in the early twenty-first century demand a new view and seriousness when it comes to shaping and maintaining the IT organization, and will consider topics such as portfolio management and the importance of customer engagement models.

In 'Solutions vs. Products' we will examine the organizational impact of moving from a product-based to a solutions-based business model. How are the various IT functions – such as operations or service delivery – effected by these changing approaches, and how can we ensure (and insure) that the IT organization is in place to meet these challenges?

'Outsourcing', in recognizing the increasing trend to place critical elements of IT's delivery capability external to the core business entity, argues that IT functions are poorly aligned to both manage these relationships and rise to the challenges that outsourcing offers. I will suggest how we can shape ourselves to address these issues.

Finally, in 'Resource Management' we go back to some fundamental questions about people. If we are to adopt a new approach to the shaping of IT organizations, then we need to recognize that we will also need to adapt resource management in the light of these. I will argue for a fresh consideration of skills, roles and accountabilities, and propose that if our new structural models are to deliver what is required we will need to take a radical approach to how we both manage and empower the people within those models.

Defining the shape of an IT organization is a serious business. It is much more that simply removing a set of components from a 'box' and laying them out in a fashion that might be esoterically pleasing but only semi-functional. And it is something we ignore at our peril.

Acknowledgements

I extend my gratitude to those whose individual insights have contributed to this book and who are acknowledged in my references. Thanks are due to my Editors at Springer for their support and encouragement during the production of this manuscript. And, as ever, the challenge of completing this book would have been so much greater without the understanding of Sarah, my wife.

If there are errors or omissions within the book then, by and large, I suspect they will be of my own making. I plead for your understanding in such cases, and hope that you will find the final article useful, elucidating and – hopefully – not a little inspiring.

Considerations for the IT Organization

1.1 Introduction

1.1.1 An Outline of the Argument

There are, without doubt, many reasons for business failure. At the most basic level the imbalance is a simple equation which offers 'profit' and 'cost' as the two primary protagonists. If businesses fail, more often than not it is because they did not make sufficient money; the weight on the 'profit' side of the equation being inadequate to ensure the required positive imbalance. There may, of course, be many contributing factors to this unsatisfactory outcome: insufficient customers, a poorly constructed product, diabolical levels of service, ambitious pricing strategies, or even a fatally flawed business idea.

Unless the product or service at the heart of the commercial model is entirely systems-related – such as a software product – the failure of an Information Technology (IT) function or project at the micro level is traditionally unlikely to have caused the demise of the entire business. Perhaps the delivery of the new financial management system was delayed or the installation of a warehousing package ran over budget, yet if business models and products are sound such failures may have caused essentially only local difficulties. Not achieving new internal efficiency targets may have added a couple of additional staff to the corporate headcount, but it would not have brought about the collapse of the enterprise. In this sense, the failure of IT projects or initiatives have – with the exception of a few very high-profile cases, such as the London Stock Exchange 'Taurus' project in the 1990s – been entirely a matter for domestic consumption.

However, as the commercial world plunges into the complexity of e-business, the importance of IT as a business critical delivery mechanism is growing. Now, if the IT project fails there may be no Internet-facing ordering system available for our customers, or the e-procurement link between ourselves and our suppliers may become unreliable resulting in inaccurate, missing or inappropriate order placement with associated knock-ons in terms of manufacturing output, product availability and so forth. Suddenly if IT fails to deliver, in many cases the business scales can be seen to perceptibly tip away from 'profit'.

The success of an IT undertaking is usually measured in terms of function, time and cost: did the project deliver what was specified, when it was supposed to, and did it cost what was forecast? Not surprisingly, therefore, success – or otherwise – is often measured in the same way: the project failed 'because it was late', 'because it was expensive', 'because it processed information three times more slowly than had been needed'. Self-evidently this is an inadequate analysis. Ask the question 'why was it late/expensive/slow?' and business and IT managers often delve a little deeper to reveal a lack of formal methodology or process, rigour or flexibility, expertise or experience.

What is seldom realized is that many projects or initiatives are impeded prior to their commencement because the very structure within which they will be executed is flawed.

An analogy: I am the manager of a Premier League football team. I have assembled the most expensive squad in the entire country and, in a recent poll of sporting journalists, it was agreed that I had the best eleven players in Europe on my side. After ten matches of the new season, my team had lost every single game. If I had such a great and incomparable line-up, how could this have happened? Simple; my team was made up entirely of attackers.

As with any similar multi-person endeavour, as team manager I needed a balance of skills, attack and defence. Not only that, I needed a way of playing, a footballing 'method', a formation. In short, an 'organization'. It may be fanciful to pursue this parallel too far, but the IT manager needs his 'way of playing', 'method' and 'formation' too – however, many do not recognize this as critical to their endeavours. If every project is undertaken with a flawed organization (no goalie or four right-wingers) then it will be more by luck than anything else if, at the end, the manager can happily state that he delivered to specification, time and budget.

My fundamental argument is that the shape of the IT organization is critical to business delivery; that it is even more fundamental than the choice of management methodology and technologies. Get the organizational shape wrong and watch as problems cascade invisibly outwards like a proverbial ripple.

1.1.2 The Purpose and Scope of an Organization

Before moving on, we should consider the purpose and scope of an organization from a broad perspective so that we have a framework for what follows. In this endeavour, the analogy of our football team – or perhaps any sporting team – may continue to prove useful. After all, in a reduction to its simplest motivations, the team is put together to win. It represents a collection of individuals who share a common objective and whose success – as a team – is measured by the achievement of that objective.

Day and Wendler (1998) were talking about business entities when they suggested that "organizations exist to motivate their members and co-ordinate their activities". This definition certainly applies to the sports team too. As manager of the football team, my role is also to motivate the individuals within the squad and, through the application of a way of playing or formation, co-ordinate their efforts on the pitch. If we can apply such an outline to either an entire business or just a football team, then it would seem to be a reasonable place to start our definition of an organization.

The study of organizations – particularly in the sphere of business – is not a new endeavour. Indeed, one of the first men to discuss organizations in academic terms was Frederick Taylor (1856–1917). Taylor's view of the purpose and scope of a business collective was the maximization of prosperity and achievement of optimum goals (see Boylan, 2001). To meet these demands, Taylor argued that management and work-force were interdependent. Whilst some of Taylor's arguments have lost a degree of credence in the recent past, these notions of achieving optimum goals and resource (role) inter-relation surely remain true.

We might choose to broaden the scope and purpose of the organization a little beyond achievement of goals (prosperity) and the management structure contained therein. I would argue that a modern-day organization is also essentially about a number of other things:

- Vision – the articulation of the future (for both business and organization)

- Leadership – as well as management – the macro, set against the micro

- Efficiency – getting as much as possible from the resource available

- Process – an approach to the execution of one's responsibilities

As a sanity check, consider the above against our football team. Our vision is to build a team capable of winning the league (objective) and then moving on to glory in European competition. Leadership is provided by the manager or coach (macro-level), the control-level management by the captain on the field of play (micro). We espouse efficiency by demanding that our strikers assist in defence when we are under attack, and that some of our defenders support the strike force when we move forwards. Our process is to pass the ball to feet, operate a 4-4-2 formation, and play the offside trap.

Of course none of this should come as any surprise to a manager either in business or team sports. Surely it is second nature? Surely we instinctively know these considerations will apply? Perhaps; but for many managers this blind naivety results in them taking organizational shape for granted and making assumptions about what will or will not happen or work in the future. More than that, when they actually consider the shape of their organization they do so from the simple perspective of it being nothing more than a reporting mechanism: a chain of command that links everyone, through one or more others, back to them. Ask a hundred managers to redefine the shape of the department where they work and over which they are to take hypothetical control, and I would expect at least ninety of them to start by drawing interconnected boxes on a sheet of paper and writing names in the spaces created. This is how they interpret organizational imperatives.

1.1.3 Why is Organizational Shape Important?

At the core of this argument is the premiss that the organization – whatever it may be – is the *only* structure available to ensure delivery against the objectives set. What one undertakes as part of a 'team' is limited, predicated and bounded by the shape of the resource available to take on the task. An orchestra that is put together to perform an Albinoni adagio recital might struggle if the programme were suddenly changed to a symphony by Bruchner. Success is possible not only through having the appropriate skills available but also skills in the right quantities.

Consider a retail business with an established customer services function. For years the business has dealt with its customer complaints via post and the telephone. Indeed, it has found that appropriately specialized staff working in two teams handle customer interaction the best, and these units have been sized to process complaints and the like as quickly as they can. In this scenario, our organizational mores of vision, efficiency and process have been clearly addressed.

With the opening of its on-line store, the business now faces a new method of customer interaction, namely e-mail. Taking the view that there is little difference between e-mail and a letter delivered through the post, the company chooses not to reorganize its customer services function in any way. The result is disaster. Enquiry turnaround times increase, complaints balloon, morale plummets. And why? Because it did not recognize that it now has three distinct streams to deal with; because its processes were unable to be adapted to address the new method of interaction; and because its resource mix – in terms of numbers of staff in each area – failed to take into account the sheer volume of Internet-based calls.

If "failure to achieve success is often the result of organizational, political and cultural issues being inadequately addressed" (Ward et al., 1990), then our simple customer services example illustrates both the first and last of the three issues suggested above. The point is that, no matter how good the staff available to the customer services manager, without ensuring that they were operating in an organization aligned to the needs of the business he was doomed to failure. It is this alignment which is critical to organizational success. The volume of resource available and their skills will be important, but if they are not aligned to the needs of the business … To our list of critical success elements – vision, leadership, efficiency and process – we should now add alignment.

But just how damaging can ineffective alignment be? If Nyström (1996) is correct when he suggests that "structure may influence strategy", then the answer is surely clear. A well-established games company possesses a highly successful product development function which has, over the years, evolved into three units each with their own particular areas of specialism: strategy games, sports games, and party games. With the coming of the Internet, the business made a successful evolution to producing versions of its games designed for computers through the addition of a whole new set of skills within its current organizational structure. Now, thanks to a highly successful motion picture, spin-off demand begins to grow for a new kind of game based around the dungeons-and-dragons theme. The business recognizes this potential market and needs to decide whether or not it should enter it aggressively. For the head of product development, whatever the business decides, he is adamant that he is not going to change an organizational structure that is proven to work.

Under these circumstances there are two potential outcomes. Firstly the business decides to enter the market, and the strategy games department is charged with developing the new product. The result is likely to be poor as a) the prerequisite skills are likely to be absent, b) this will deflect from what the department is really good at so product quality suffers, c) business reputation begins to fall in consequence, and so on. The second outcome is where the business looks at its organization and the way it is aligned, and simply says 'we don't do that'. It loses out on a lucrative new product area and its market share begins to fall. This latter scenario – 'we don't do that' – is perhaps one of the major inhibiting factors in the IT space when it comes to the strategic alignment of the technical function with the business it is there to serve.

1.2 The Issue

1.2.1 The IT Organization: Is It a Special Case?

Undoubtedly much that can be said in terms of organizational theory applies not only to the IT function but also to other individual departments right through to the highest level of the largest international corporation. The 'father' of such study, Henri Fayol (1841–1925) in his 'Administration Industrielle et Generale' (1916) outlined the purpose and scope of an organization as the need to plan, to organize, to command, to co-ordinate, and to control (see Boylan, 2001). Like Taylor, whilst some elements of Fayol's theory have become less fashionable of late, much of the basic framework remains sound. Turning the supposition on its head, where is the manager who wants to preside over an organization that is unplanned, disorganized, anarchic, unco-ordinated and lacking any kind of governance?

For the IT function striving to articulate its vision and objectives, and to deliver efficiently against a predictable process, the aspects of planning, co-ordination and so forth must also be facilitated by the organization that is put in place. Indeed, one might argue that we are beginning to build a series of checkpoints against which the efficacy of the organization might be measured:

- Is there a clearly stated vision?

- Is the organization headed by a strong and visible leader?

- Are there efficient processes and procedures that govern the organization?

- Is there an overall organizational plan?

- Is the command structure clear and unambiguous?

But – you might query – how does this list (which could be considerably longer) apply differently to an IT function in comparison with, say, the Finance function or the Manufacturing facility? Broadly speaking it does not; but where it does distinguish itself is in the area of alignment.

Let us consider a business comprising of a number of discrete elements: Product Development, Manufacturing and Logistics, Sales and Marketing, Customer Services, Finance, Human Resources (HR), and Information Technology. Of these, the first four – whilst inter-related – have function-specific goals as their objectives; from developing new products, through their manufacture and selling, then on to pre- and post-sales customer support. The remaining three departments offer services to the business as a whole. The Finance function is essentially charged with managing the company's money, and though interfacing with all other areas can structure itself to best meet its local goals. In Human Resources the picture is similar. Although every other function is dependent on them, the HR 'product' is consistent across the organization and they can therefore organize themselves to best suit delivery of that product.

IT faces the most difficult conundrum. While it might be relatively straightforward to articulate elements of vision, process and co-ordination, the issue of alignment complicates the picture. It would be reasonable to assume that all its partner departments are seeking the same kind of service from their IT colleagues. However, it would also be reasonable to assume that each of these departments not only works in their own particular way (process and governance) but also has some discrete systems requirements (objectives) and is uniquely organized to best meet their local challenges. Thus the structure of the HR function is likely to be very different from that in Manufacturing or Sales. Given that the staff within the IT organization must interface with each of these different models or shapes – as well as putting in place something which allows it to manage itself effectively – I would argue that it is here where one of the fundamental challenges for IT organizations lay.

1.2.2 Traditional IT Organizational Models

The bulk of IT functions not unnaturally turn inwards when it comes to defining their organizations. Priorities tend to be set by the infrastructure and applications that they need to manage, perhaps influenced by the governance or process models chosen to support them overall. At the least granular level we might typically find a department split into two basic areas – 'applications' or 'development', and 'operations' – with other functions – such as the help desk or 'Project Office' – resident in or alongside these. The structure within each discrete element is likely to be similar, driven by a basic hierarchical premiss and the need for formal control.

Where these organizations may differ is in their alignment. If we expand on the business outlined in the previous section (I'll call it Acme Global) we can demonstrate how – using traditional thinking – the IT function can be moulded in various ways.

First some further detail: The products produced by Acme Global are organized into three distinct groups based upon the market sectors at which they are aimed. This split is broadly mirrored in the manufacturing function with the exception of an additional fourth unit that produces some components common to all three product groupings. Given that the company has an international reach, the Sales function is structured to reflect this with six regional UK units plus a single unit in each of ten European countries. Both Marketing and Logistics are UK-based with a nominated contact in each offshore business. There are single functions in each country (including the UK) for Customer Services and Human Resources, sized to meet the needs of the local business and reflecting the UK's position as Head Office.

As far as the IT department is concerned, there are a limited number of support staff outside the UK, again dependant upon the size of the operation in each territory. Three core applications are run out of the UK in the areas of Manufacturing, Enterprise Resource Planning (ERP; including both Finance and Logistics) and Customer Relationship Management (CRM). The first two of these run on IBM and DB2 technology, the CRM system on Oracle and Unix. In addition to various interfaces between these systems, some functions – such as HR – run other specialized systems. In some countries there are also additional software packages and infrastructure technologies, and in some instances these are used in preference to the central system.

Whilst complex, this would not be an untypical scenario for a multinational organization. The key question is how should this landscape influence the structure of the IT organization? If we assume that the IT Director chooses to follow the simple application/operations split, how might his organization look? Let us briefly consider the two most obvious options.

A Systems-based Organization

In the applications area the IT Director builds his structure around the three core applications with dedicated teams to support the Manufacturing, ERP and CRM systems. The smaller systems will be supported either within one of these core teams or by one (or more) units dedicated to those systems. From the operations perspective, support is provided through teams with specific expertise – e.g. in DB2, Unix and Oracle – in addition to a help desk function which majors on desktop systems and associated software. There is a specialist networks function that manages the local, UK and international communications requirements. Support for businesses outside of the UK is provided through resource allocated to these core teams and is delivered on an ad-hoc basis as appropriate.

Whilst this structure will meet the bulk of the function's responsibilities from a pure systems perspective, it does throw up a number of challenges and problems. For example:

- The ERP development team has two distinct user communities to serve. There may be difficulties in ensuring appropriate engagement and work prioritization between these business units.

- Some of the smaller systems could be starved of support if resource allocated to them is primarily focused on one of the 'big three' applications.

- Management of an effective relationship with the international operations could prove problematic, particularly when providing part-time support from UK resource that is not fluent in 'local' configurations.

- The help desk – by being based in the operations area and very desktop-focused – may not work well with the applications team providing support to critical business applications. Some frictions may arise within the IT community.

- For many users, it may be difficult to see clearly with whom they should interface in the event of a problem arising.

A Business-based Organization

In this scenario, the IT Director chooses to keep his operations organization more or less as defined for the systems-based example above. The key difference is in the area of the help desk where he has chosen to identify a primary contact for each business department as well as two resources to fulfil the same role for the international locations. Within applications he has set up six development teams (of varying sizes), each focused on a specific business function, e.g. Sales, HR, and so on. In addition, he has also established a small team of 'international consultants' whose remit is to manage the systems and interfaces of the non-UK business and ensure that there is compliance with the overall group IT strategy.

As before, such an approach will have benefits in terms of providing direct links between IT and the business, but it also has difficulties:

- Given the support for key groups of ERP system users through two discrete teams, there is a danger of overlap, duplication and problems with co-ordination when it comes to the development of this system.

- Some areas of the business – e.g. HR – may not warrant a dedicated IT resource to look after them, and this may prove an expensive luxury for the function.

- With the establishment of six business-IT relationships, the potential exists for the abandonment or circumvention of 'standard' IT processes and procedures in an effort to improve or tailor services for a specific group of users. This could occur in both development and help desk areas.

- The pool of international consultants will need to be carefully monitored, justified and controlled to ensure that they are providing real value-add for the business as a whole. This could prove to be an expensive 'white elephant'.

These are simple illustrations, and I have deliberately chosen to largely ignore the operations area when suggesting issues in the two scenarios above.

1.2.3 So Where Does the Problem in IT Organizations Lie?

In our significantly reduced analysis above we can see examples of how an IT organization put in place to address alignment issues from one particular perspective can throw up challenges in another. As illustrations, these two outline scenarios begin to suggest the depth and complexity of IT organizational definition. In many instances it will be the

Table 1.1. The Organizational Objectives Matrix

	Planning	Organization	Command	Control	Governance
Vision	?	✓	✗	✗	✗
Leadership	?	✗	✓	✓	?
Efficiency	?	✗	✗	✓	✓
Process	?	✗	✗	✓	✓
Alignment	?	✓	✗	✗	✗

failure to recognize either depth or complexity (if not both!) which contributes significantly to problems that may effectively remain hidden. Indeed, where this is the case, IT managers will see the symptoms of this underlying flaw in a plethora of processes or process work-arounds, a high-level of problem escalation to the top tiers of the IT management structure, and end-user meetings where the IT function always seems to send a cast of thousands.

If we consider macro organizational objectives as a matrix, we can also immediately identify areas of compatibility and conflict (see Table 1.1).

In this matrix, boxes have been ticked where there are obvious compatibilities between prime organizational drivers. However, a box that is not ticked effectively represents a challenge for the IT manager, i.e. how does he ensure that alignment and control are 'compatible'? Ideally he will need to put in place an IT organization in such a way as to ensure that these issues are addressed. For example, one might argue that in delivering a vision for the IT organization, it should be possible to define organizational shape plus elements of planning; command, control and governance are not, however, fundamentally influenced by the vision. Alignment also has a clear relationship with organizational shape as its primary driver, and it can also significantly influence planning (e.g. through business-focused change programmes); however, the alignment model adopted will tend to be independent of day-to-day methods of command, control and governance. Seen from the other angle, the planning objective is potentially effected by all its matrix partners, though specifically 'matched' with none.

Through this kind of analysis we can see how issues may arise in situations where, as in the case of planning, there is no clear owner or driver, and where some elements – as with control and governance – may find themselves influenced by owners or drivers with potentially conflicting

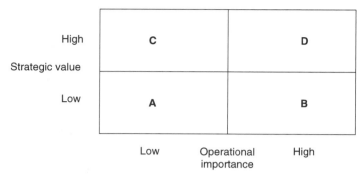

Figure 1.1. *Strategic Value vs. Operational Importance*

motivations, e.g. the leadership notion of control may run counter to that espoused by efficiency objectives. Furthermore, conflicts can be exacerbated in those IT functions where the matrix elements have individuals who are explicitly responsible for one or more of them. For example, in order to establish the specific method of control, the leadership owner/driver may require an organization that effectively runs counter to that outlined by the vision.

Another way of identifying the kinds of issue implicit in the shaping of an IT organization is to consider the strategic value of systems and applications against their operational importance. Barton (2002) suggests a Boston matrix to illustrate his point (see Figure 1.1).

Barton argues that each element of the IT infrastructure sits within one of the four boxes, A through to D. Through analysis of the numbers of applications and/or systems sitting in each box, one is able to draw certain conclusions about the position of IT systems in relation to business innovation. From the perspective of shaping the IT organization the model is also useful to assist with our analysis of structural problems within traditional IT functions. The 'systems' in quadrant D, for example, will be the most critical to the business and, by implication, the teams that support those systems represent the greatest area of resource risk to the business. There is an argument, therefore, to ensure an appropriate degree of focus on this resource – and the organization of that resource. There is also a further argument to suggest that there could be some benefit in recognizing that the way systems in group A are supported could be different from those in the other groups, particularly group D. However, traditional IT organizations may fail to recognize this kind of distinction and impose a standard model across all systems –

irrespective of where they might be located – expecting uniform results and consistent degrees of success from each.

1.2.4 Aims of this Book

Our theoretical examples above begin to uncover some of the underlying challenges which, for many, remain undiscovered in their IT organizations. As I have said, not only are they undiscovered, they can also invisibly detract from the chance of successful delivery against the function's overall objectives. Part of this book's intent is to peel back the covers of organizational veneer. We must delve a little beneath the surface of the organization chart to reveal exactly what lies there.

Doing this in isolation is not enough, however. We should also address some current trends both in terms of business drivers and IT supply theory, the latter most obviously manifest in the inexorable movement towards outsourcing and utility computing. Both this fashion and the growing importance of elements such as e-business initiatives or the focus on cash and return on investment (ROI) should also be reflected in the IT organizational models. In cases such as these we need both to identify the influence and then to suggest how appropriate organization can not only mitigate against the challenges introduced but also enhance the benefit to be gained. For example, e-business initiatives may demand a fast and flexible systems delivery model to maximize its business impact – but how should we structure our function in order to best meet this kind of need?

To help tackle this analysis, we will also consider variations on organizational theory in addition to those of Fayol and Taylor already mentioned. Although not specifically aimed at the IT function, we have already seen how general arguments can help to provide us with differing perspectives on the shape of systems departments. Indeed, in considering a statement such as this from Ward et al. (1990) – "it is most critical that the IS [Information Systems] organization is structured to satisfy its customers' requirements as well as manage itself effectively" – I have already demonstrated that what may be self-evident is not necessarily the same as that which is simple.

In some respects, therefore, the book is attempting a little detective work. Where are there real or potential issues in IT organizations? What puzzles do the modern business environment present to us? Then, in attempting to answer these questions, we will consider possible solutions. How should our IT function be aligned with the business? What are the benefits of central control over distributed responsibility? Indeed, are the two both compatible and necessary? Finally, if organizations are about people – their fundamental component – then what considerations must we observe in this sphere?

My objective is for this book to provide a vehicle for reconsideration of the IT organization; a stimulus for looking afresh at how we construct the framework within which systems delivery is undertaken. Hopefully some of the suggestions will be challenging; some will certainly be difficult to implement; not all will apply to every company's IT function. The justification? Ask yourself one question: Is there anything about your IT organization which you would like to change and which would improve its contribution to the business? Only if you answered 'No' are you allowed to close the book and return to the comfort of your padded cell!

1.3 Key Considerations for IT

1.3.1 Organizational Strategy

Before moving on to examine the prevalent forms of organization within a traditional IT function, there are a number of influencing themes that we need to touch on to ensure that our future perspective is a rounded one. To some of these topics – such as outsourcing or the question of the IT 'product' – I will be returning in a little more detail later. The subjects are:

- Organizational strategy
- Quality and reliability of service
- Flexibility and proactivity
- Value for money and ROI
- Integrating with 'the business'
- The imperatives that drive business change
- The imperatives that drive IT change
- The impact of outsourcing and e-business

One might wish to point out that the first of these is really what this present investigation is all about, and indeed that is so. However, we need to recognize that organizational strategy is not something that can be decided in isolation. It operates at the most macro of levels against other strategies and corporate decision-making.

During a study of the Swedish company, EKA Nobell, Harry Nyström exposed the kind of generic conflicts that can influence how we approach our organizational models (Nyström, 1996). For example, much in the IT realm is about delivering change into an enterprise. By definition, we can reasonably argue that this must imply some kind of inherent metamorphosis within the business itself, e.g. in the way it supports the products it sells, perhaps. Organizational shape is – traditionally, at least – partly about defining a resource matrix that provides a degree of stability and certainty within which people can function effectively. Is there not therefore an immediate dichotomy here in the attempt to overlay something that does not change across a business that is, to some degree or other, in a constant state of flux? What does this demand of our organizational shape if not the suppleness – and subtleness – to be able to bend with the business it serves?

In a 'chicken and egg' scenario, we face similar questions around strategy, be it business or (more practically) IT strategy. The question here is, does strategy drive structure or vice versa? If we have an IT function that is organized in a particular way, then it is likely that we will implement strategies that can readily be supported and delivered by that structure. Who would want to attempt to implement a strategy that is known to be immediately compromised by an inability to deliver against it? Conversely one can argue that strategy dictates structure. If there is a wish to implement a particular new technology – content management, for example – and the present IT structure has no logical 'home' for this initiative, then should the structure not change to accommodate it? The point in both of these examples is simply to illustrate that we should not attempt to implement any organizational shape on the basis that it is 'right', fits a textbook model, or will deliver absolutely anything that is required. In the new economy, our IT organization must be malleable – open to the influences of both strategy and change – otherwise it will fail.

There will be global considerations too. At the corporate level, some themes or cultural behaviours will be expected to apply to all functions within the enterprise. For example, there may be a suggestion that a single-status organization with a culture of passion (Bell, 2002) is critical to the success of most resource-driven endeavours. Such tenets may be the bedrock upon which the success of an international conglomerate is based – and if so, then the expectations will be that these models are replicated in the IT function too. So when it comes to organizational strategy, we should appreciate that shaping the IT function is not simply a case of adopting the 'best' model and sticking to it. There are powerful forces at work that will ensure that an ability to adapt – if not to compromise, in some instances – is a prerequisite.

1.3.2 Quality and Reliability of Service

In the same way as one might initially wish to question our inclusion of those 'strategic' elements, above, the notion that quality and reliability of service are also influencers of any IT organizational shape may seem unlikely. After all, one could surely argue that the quality and reliability of the services provided from within an IT function are about 'how' the job is done rather than the way resources are organized. That service quality is increasingly important is almost a non sequitur, as Brittain and Matlus have pointed out: "as enterprises become increasingly dependent on IT, they demand a higher quality of service" (Brittain and Matlus, 2002).

Yet quality and reliability reside not only within the realm of network server performance or the code within any suite of application software modules. There is no intrinsic right to expect to achieve acceptable levels of service just because one has purchased the 'best' components. Simple examples will show how both quality and reliability can be impacted by the way in which we choose to define our organizational model.

Let us assume that we have implemented an Enterprise Resource Planning (ERP) system that is widely regarded as the most robust and high-performing in its class. We have also ensured that our in-house resources have been rigorously trained and accredited to enable them to modify or enhance the system as appropriate. Despite having all the necessary package-related skills, if we do not have in place the prerequisite generic IT skills – such as Business Analysis or Project Management expertise – or a resource structure which supports a thorough application development life cycle, then there is a possibility that – directly as a result of our organizational approach – we are in danger of delivering additional business function which is not as specified, does not reach an acceptable level of quality, and is implemented late and over budget.

Some of this is plainly obvious, but does serve to suggest the interdependency of our organizational functions. Similarly with our best-in-class network servers; if there is a problem with one of them, how do we manage this? Not only should there be a high-quality process sitting behind appropriate teams to rectify the problem, but we should also have a suitable means of engaging with our business customers – such as through a help desk – to enable us to manage inquiries, complaints and so forth. If we do not, then our organization may force our customers to interrupt the very people who are supposed to be fixing their problems, thereby impeding our ability to resolve issues and impacting the overall service. If we must build quality in to the entire IT product, then the organization should be aligned to support that delivery too.

1.3.3 Flexibility of Response; Being Proactive

We have already indicated that "strategic change may lead to structural change" (Nyström, 1996), and perhaps nowhere is this better indicated than in the technology-led aspects of early twenty-first century business life. The Internet – and Internet-based e-business applications – have raised the bar for enterprises in terms of their strategic readiness to respond. In previous systems generations, lead times for business initiatives could potentially be measured in years rather than, as now, in weeks if not days. Competitive advantage was something sought – and delivered – over the medium- to long-term.

Particularly in relation to Business-to-Consumer (B2C) companies, the Internet has both enabled and thus driven the shortening of business initiative timeframes. For IT functions within those companies, associated delivery timescales have tightened too (along with, somewhat paradoxically, an increased demand for quality of end product). From an organizational perspective we should recognize that there is therefore a need for a parallel and supportive shift. IT structures based around technologies, projects and programmes with long life cycles are in danger of proving a significant barrier to the kind of flexibility and speed of response that businesses now demand. In order to meet the new calls for rapid delivery, not only will there be an impact on the organizational structures themselves, but we can also expect to see a knock-on effect in process- and management-related areas. This demand for flexibility also echoes the problem of the change–stability dichotomy referred to a little earlier.

But the challenge is not just in terms of IT coming to recognize and adopt a more flexible and responsive way of managing itself; there is also a new challenge for people residing within those structures. Bell recognizes the need for "selecting, motivating and developing employees with the requisite skills and demonstrated behaviours to operate effectively in a highly uncertain, highly unstructured environment" (Bell, 2002). These people represent a new breed of individual who are capable of operating within a semi-structured organization, and who thrive on the demands likely to be placed upon them in terms of an emphasis on proactivity and flexibility. The 'my job is X, and I do X' needs to be replaced with a philosophy that states 'my role is X, though I have the skills to do Y – and, if called upon, I can do Z as well'. As we shall increasingly discover, an even greater emphasis is being placed on the *kinds* of people residing within the IT function as opposed to the more traditional – if not regimented – notion that structure and skills were all-important.

1.3.4 Value for Money; Good Return on Investment

There has, of course, always been a latent demand that IT investments 'pay their way'. Until recently, this latency existed because the most significant of projects tended to run over a considerable time-span and/or consumed such significant amounts of resource (people and money) that any form of benefit measurement proved almost impossible. This may have been partly due to the fragile nature of some of the business cases put together to justify the IT spend – assuming that any such concrete justification was forthcoming in the first place!

Recently, however, there has been growing pressure within enterprises to ensure that investments made do indeed bring worthwhile payback. As Beck suggests, "user organizations are ... attempting to define the elusive business value they desperately seek from their IT assets" (Beck, 2002). This increased focus has arisen for a number of reasons, such as:

- The economic climate of the early twenty-first century, with ripples of recession being felt in both Europe and the USA, has forced corporate executives to look more seriously at where their money goes. In many organizations, detailed business cases for IT spend have become the norm, with hard-edged benefits being sought from both the IT function and the user community served.

- Projects have, in terms of resource consumption, become smaller and therefore – in theory at least – easier to track and manage. ROI on a six-man-month project is likely to be more readily definable than on something ten or twenty times that size.

- IT initiatives which are e-business focused lend themselves to measurement of concrete benefit after a very short period indeed. Applications may be introduced on a pilot basis, the decision as to their rollout being dependent on how that system performs in the commercial arena. Indeed, some Internet businesses will have their entire commercial ethos and survival effectively based around the delivery of IT services.

Within the IT function, this presents a difficult problem, particularly as the benefits to be gained are most likely to be seen outside of the systems function and therefore the responsibility of other managers to deliver. Despite that – and almost to justify their existence perhaps – "CIOs [Chief Information Officers] are still chasing after some measurable ROI while struggling to translate the demands of their businesses into effective IT strategies" (Beck, 2002).

Coming under the microscope like this has a unique impact on the IT organization. Increasingly IT directors and managers are being asked to justify their functional structures not just at the project level but at the resource level too. Thus, the question of 'where is the payback on this project?' is being broadened out to 'what value-add does this resource bring to the organization?' This trend can most evidently be seen within the equation that balances the cost of the internal resource against that likely to be incurred from outsourcing that same skill, role or function. Indeed, the demand for cost-effective IT service provision with solid ROI – essentially based on the cost of the IT organization – has probably been the prime driver for outsourcing initiatives.

1.3.5 Being an Integral Part of the Business

Whether we like it or not, the IT functions of many companies have remained somewhat aloof, outside of the mainstream business community. Undoubtedly many of the reasons for this are historical, perhaps based on the practices adopted by embryonic computing departments. Indeed, even when IT managers began to wake up to this issue of exclusion – IT from the business, the business from IT – the approaches taken to supposedly bridge the divide are initiated by technical people, and based around project processes and essentially technical metalanguage.

For example, the drive in the latter part of the last century to place a greater emphasis on project initiation brought with it a series of workshops, meetings, reports, forms, calculations and procedures, all of which were designed to help outline the project, programme or initiative from an IT perspective. The aim was often to justify and define the work to be carried out in IT systems- or project-centric terms. What this kind of approach failed to recognize (even though it was a valuable step forwards in many respects) was that the vast majority of business users – or IT's 'customers' – were process-based and not truly project literate. Their sense of the importance of an issue and their means of articulating it were not enveloped in systems methodology or project-logic; they understood their everyday process problems, issues and complaints in their own terms and based on the way they did their jobs.

This failure to communicate was, inevitably, only partly addressed by the new initiation focus. Indeed, subsequent attempts to integrate IT into the business have – albeit unconsciously – largely followed similar lines. IT managers have tried to tie themselves into the business cycle through the adoption of mechanisms such as the 'programme board' or the 'engagement manager'; there is talk about 'account management' too. For the vast majority, these are once again simply variations on the same theme: approaches to communication which are predicated on the ground rules, process and language of the IT function.

Recent changes in the business landscape – for example, via the Internet – and the obvious implications to be faced subsequently in the IT delivery model, have only really exacerbated this trend. In many enterprises the need to understand what IT really brings to the business, the desire to see "guarantee delivered value" (Foote et al., 2001), are symptoms of the gap that still exists. For many in the systems community this chasm represents something of a blind spot. If there are Engagement Managers, Project Initiation Workshops, Programme Boards and well-defined processes, how can there possibly be a problem?

In shaping the IT organization we need to recognize this theme as a real issue that IT managers must address. New business models demand a closer union between the IT function and the business it is supposed to serve. With commercial success ever more tightly dependant on the successful coupling of the IT–business partnership, implementing an organization that merely has the right kinds of roles defined within it to supposedly marry with the user community – these supported by some Prince-type structures – simply will not suffice.

1.3.6 The Shift in Business Emphasis

The influence of this latter element – the new business models – is what takes the communication imperative to another realm. If the IT–business disjoin were simply a matter of communication failure then it is entirely possible that other incremental steps would suffice to somewhat bridge the gap. For example, if the mechanism, language and processes that lie behind project initiation workshops, programme boards and the like, were moulded more towards a business focus, then the engagement might prove a little more fruitful. What makes the IT community need to look beyond such small advances is the step-change being imposed upon enterprises themselves.

Take Business Process Reengineering (BPR) for example. Ten or fifteen years ago, BPR was in many respects much more mechanistic than systemic. It was possible at that time to make significant improvements through changes in existing manual processes, and support these with some kind of systems enhancement or development. In the vast majority of cases for the systems community this was just a supporting role. Even adoption of Electronic Data Interchange (EDI) in large corporate organizations was more about speeding up existing mechanisms rather than responding to radical changes in business models.

If, as Dreyfuss (2002) suggests, "today, business processes are intended to give an enterprise market advantage", then this is because modern BPR is likely to be significantly more radical and far more dependant in IT than in the past. We could consider Amazon as a case in point. When Amazon launched their Internet-based book-selling proposition, they broke the mould. Here was not only a new way of dealing with customers; Amazon.com represented a new business model, new processes and ways of working, all dependent on IT. To reiterate: not supported by, but entirely dependent on IT. For competitors in this commercial space, limited BPR with tweaks in existing processes or systems would have plainly been inadequate to meet the challenge. This kind of shift, driven by a new business imperative, effectively means that a 'small advance' in business–IT interfacing is simply not enough.

Mahoney (2001) suggests a number of key business drivers that have shifted the emphasis in business terms – and therefore in the way that IT must respond, such as:

- mergers and acquisitions – the growing challenge of integrating disparate businesses, models and systems

- the connected economy – such as shared supply chain models and new ways to approach customer integration

- e-business – not only examples such as Amazon, but also business developments which may have spawned new departments or divisions and thus new ways of working

- outsourcing – and the new complexities and issues that this brings forward

All of these drivers have one thing in common: namely that the IT function supporting the business which is facing these changes must change too – and that some of these changes must be around organizational shape. Only then can it fulfil the new expectations that are being placed upon it.

1.3.7 The Game has Changed

From the perspective of a business–IT relationship my argument is that, in the very recent past, the game has radically changed – and the rules by which that game is played have metamorphosed into something else. The pressures of flexibility and proactivity, the need for solid ROI and appropriate engagement with the business community, are all spin-offs from the shift in business emphasis which need a fresh approach from the IT function.

The assertion that at the heart of the new proposition is the challenge of "creating high-value solutions by integrating various products and services – even merging the supplier's and customer's operations – to solve a complete customer problem" (Foote et al., 2001) cries out for something other than 'more of the same' from IT. Indeed, there are a number of key notions within this very quote which suggest as much: "solutions", "integrating", "merging", "supplier's operations", "customer's operations" and "customer problem". In the realm where the current methods and organizational models were drawn up, many of these notions were either not a consideration or meant something completely different, as summarized in Table 1.2.

If this is not enough to recognize that a shift-change is required from IT, then we can add to the argument that there are new deliverables demanded of the systems function. Consider the statement that "the challenge of IT has shifted from delivering information to exploiting it" (Beck, 2002). Such a proposition requires an entirely new way of seeing

Table 1.2. The New Business Imperatives

	Late 20th century	Early 21st century
Solutions	Tending to mean the delivery of a single system to meet a collection of related business needs (e.g. the implementation of a new Finance system).	Now with the connotation of a much more complex 'bundle' of deliverables including not only a systems element (potentially spread across a number of delivery platforms), but also process change and a variety of interfaces which may well go beyond the parent organization.
Integrating	Building automated interfaces between in-house systems, thereby allowing the accelerated flow of information (e.g. between core systems, EDI platforms, etc.).	More likely to have to be considered in the light of the 'solution', above, i.e. not only those internal components, but also a myriad of new or 'alternative' technologies, processes and entities.
Merging	Historically not considered.	A very real issue where the deliverable is a solution that is a collaborative effort between essentially independent business partners (e.g. in a highly integrated joint supply chain solution).
Supplier's operations	Historically not considered. 'Suppliers' for the IT function were those organizations that provided hardware and software. The integral operations of suppliers to the business as a whole were irrelevant.	Now, where a successful system delivery is reliant on effective interfacing with a supplier's operational systems (as in an e-business supply chain) those within IT need to engage with and understand these suppliers almost as much as their internal colleagues.
Customer's operations	Historically not considered.	As for the supplier's operations above. In some business propositions, this would been even more critical of course.
Customer problem	Historically not considered in the same way as now. A 'customer problem' would have been a systems issue within the parent organization.	A business customer's problems can now be only resolved by the IT function in many instances (e.g. issues with an Internet shopping cart module).

too. Thus, from an organization whose primary function revolved around the management of information – and where the emphasis was on the technology ('IT', after all) – there is the move towards the understanding and interpretation of that data as knowledge. Thus systems delivery has become not only IT but also 'IS' (Information Systems), 'IM' (Information Management) and 'KM' (Knowledge Management). How can this portfolio not require a new organization to support it and engage with the business community?

1.3.8　The Impact of Outsourcing and e-Business

Without question, one of the major IT trends currently in vogue is that of outsourcing. Subcontracting of systems service and provisioning outside of the parent organization is something we shall consider in greater depth a little later. For now we should at least recognize the scale and scope of the initiative. As reported by Beck (2002), "Gartner projects that nearly half of Fortune 1000 global enterprises will choose not to own their IT assets, but instead will derive business benefits from shared IT utility infrastructures owned and operated by service provider hybrids". Such a projection is clearly testament to the importance that outsourcing will play, not only now, but in the immediate future. After all, once outsourcing has been committed to, there is likely to be a relatively long cycle if one is to later 'insource' – primarily driven by contract agreement and resourcing considerations.

However, outsourcing in itself has also moved on: "motivations for outsourcing are evolving from a primary focus on cost reduction to an emerging emphasis on improving business performance" (Diromualdo, 1998). Thus the prime financial driver is being supplemented in addressing such elements as 'integrating', 'supplier operations' and 'customer problems' as defined in the previous section. In this, the IT manager faces a dual complexity: not only in recognizing and responding to new business drivers, but also in the need to manage solutions provision outside of his local domain. For many, outsourcing will be regarded as just something else to be managed, arguing that it is little different from any other project or supplier relationship. But as we shall argue in more detail in Chapter 5, adoption of outsourcing is another driver for the IT manager to respond with appropriate changes in his internal structure.

e-Business is little different in this regard. We have already seen how new business propositions such as Amazon.com force changes on businesses and, because of a new reliance on IT provisioning, on systems functions too. On might argue that "speed and agility are everything, because nothing is certain and change is constant" (Beck, 2002) is something of a truism, and that it has always been thus – but the new commercial imperatives make such a position more relevant today than ever before.

It is important to recognize that this speed and agility does not simply refer to computer hardware or networks (the 'IT'), but also to the applications and their associated processes (the 'IS'), and to the manipulation of information in such a way as to better enable quick and well-founded intelligent business decisions (the 'IM' and 'KM'). People will be responsible for delivering a greater proportion of the overall solution than ever before, and thus we can argue that the shape of the organization that supports IT, IS, IM and KM is critical.

What is an Organization? 2

2.1 Forms of Organization

2.1.1 The Problem with Organization Charts

In order to provide further context, in this chapter I am going to consider some generic perspectives around the organization. This will include a brief analysis on types of structure (hierarchical versus flat organizations), the difference between management and leadership, and then some other cultural elements. We will then go on to consider organizational components that are particular to the IT function, before concluding the chapter with an analysis of the organizational life cycle.

However, in advance of these discussions I would like to make a general point about an 'organization' as it is generally perceived and depicted, i.e. through an 'organogram' or organization chart. These diagrams try to do two things. Firstly they are used to represent a management structure or chain of command; it should be possible for any individual to locate themselves within the chart and then trace the various lines of management right through to the single individual who sits atop the whole enterprise. Secondly, organograms are also used to depict job descriptions. Each box on the chart will – more often than not – be labelled with a job title as well as the name of the individual who holds that position. Thus we can see that Bill is an Analyst, Joe a Programmer, and so forth. These are the jobs they do and the role they perform in the company. On this basis we would not expect Joe to act as a Team Leader nor Andy – whose title is Programme Director – to work in an administration support capacity.

Of these two aims, organization charts succeed in terms of providing a view of the management hierarchy and – I must argue – fail completely in the definition of roles and responsibilities as we must now come to view them. As I have already suggested – and as we will continue to see throughout our discussions – there is a need for a new approach to the

IT organization not only in terms of structure but also with respect to role definition. The business demand for IT to be fast and flexible can hardly be met if Joe the Programmer is *organizationally* prevented from making an even more valuable contribution to the business as a direct result of how he is defined in the formal depiction of that organization. We need to make a distinction between line management and role; and within role, we need to be mindful of the real difference between job titles and the functions that an individual may carry out. Titles are too narrow, and dangerously restrictive and misleading. We need to think about a new way of defining actual functions and responsibilities either alongside or separate from the traditional line management/job title diagrams. (I will return to this theme in Chapter 6.)

2.1.2 Hierarchical vs. Flat

It can be readily argued that there is a clear relationship between organizational structure and the way in which the organization performs and behaves (e.g. Ward et al., 1990). Broadly speaking, there are two fundamental types of construct, each with its own consequential strengths and weaknesses.

The hierarchical organization is one that tends to possess many layers of management within which control, process and measurement are prevalent. There is a clear chain of command and escalation, and structures such as these resist flexibility not only inherently but also in terms of movement across functions. For individuals, "in hierarchical forms of organization … a degree of personal initiative is sacrificed in the interest of co-operation" (Day and Wendler, 1998). As we have already seen in our examination of new IT drivers, some elements of initiative – allied with flexibility and responsiveness – can be key to success. The hierarchical organization may suppress these qualities in people.

Flat structures, on the other hand, lend themselves more towards innovation and change; there is likely to be a far greater degree of cross-functional interaction at the cost of some elements of control, clarity and process. Rosabeth Moss Kanter (1943–) argued that, for many enterprises, "empowering strategies are necessary, leading to a flatter hierarchy, decentralized authority and autonomous work groups" (Boylan, 2001). Such strategies would indeed meet the demands placed upon the organization by some business goals, but the looseness of such structures – with some loss of control that this implies – is likely to mean that other drivers would be left unsatisfied: the accurate measurement of

Table 2.1. Organizational Forms

	Some strengths ...	Some weaknesses ...
Hierarchical	Control and command; measurement; process; clear accountability	Lack of flexibility, innovation, flair, and creativity; can be impersonal; does not encourage taking responsibility
Flat	Flexibility, innovation, communication	Potential confusion over ownership; lack of process and control; can lead to 'buck passing'
Matrix	Virtual team working; task or goal focus; potentially unlocks some very flexible skill-sets	Lack of clear accountability, responsibility and ownership; prioritization issues can arise for individuals
Multi-skilled	Good in an operational support environment; ideal for fire-fighting; can create dynamic teams	Focus may be poor; potentially leads to internal conflicts over seniority; responsibility and ownership can be problematic

ROI, for example, or the need to follow formal and rigid process and procedures when dealing with interfaces to operations outside of the parent environment.

It seems self-evident then that assertions for either hierarchical or flat organization structures within the IT function will guarantee little in terms of successful delivery. That there is a need for something more has already been recognized in the arguments for variant structures such as the 'matrix' model – flexible and ideal in a task- or goal-oriented environment – or the 'multi-skilled' organization, which is perhaps best suited to support-type operations. Table 2.1 summarizes the pros and cons of these structures.

Given the breadth of the responsibility of the modern day IT function, we can reasonably argue that for most a mix of all the above structural styles will be needed. Exact compositions will vary from environment to environment, being very much business goal dependent. Yet once again I must argue that the fundamental inadequacy of the organogram still remains, even if it is clearly composed of a recipe of the four structural styles outlined above.

2.1.3 Management vs. Leadership

There is another potential dichotomy which has a significant impact on both the structure and effectiveness of the IT function in any specific business environment, and this is based around the style of the department head. As with the default 'flat' or 'hierarchical' organizational structures, there is a parallel question to be asked in terms of management and leadership. Not only are these two clearly different aspects of executing functional responsibility, they can spawn specific types of organizational structures and styles of execution that may, or may not, prove to be successful.

Charles Handy (1932–), in his book *Gods of Management*, defined four basic styles of management (see Boylan, 2001):

- "Zeus" – which operates a power-oriented, non-bureaucratic management style

- "Apollo" – where the approach would tend to be ordered and structured, with clearly defined rules and hierarchies

- "Athena" – a problem-solving style with a focus on enterprise, achievement and teamwork

- "Dionysus" – a style based on individualism and the personality of the manager

We can readily see how these styles might map onto particular organizational structures. For example, in situations where the manager's style is akin to Zeus, they are likely to put in place a structure that reflects that approach; namely something hierarchical. This is probably true for Apollo too. Athena, on the other hand, is likely to favour a matrix structure, while Dionysus would almost certainly prefer a flat organization. It is not unreasonable to argue, therefore, that the shape of the IT organization (or, indeed, any organization) is likely to be driven to a significant extent by the managerial style of the person at its head; potentially this could prove to be a greater influence on it than the demands placed upon the function by business.

In a similar way to Handy, Henry Mintzberg (1939–) considered the 'managerial' from the perspective of the kinds of role that the manager needs to perform. From Mintzberg's perspective, there are three key managerial approaches which will effectively be demanded by commercial or business imperatives (see Boylan, 2001):

Table 2.2. Management Roles vs. Management Types

Roles / Types	Interpersonal: figurehead, leader	Informational: monitoring, spokesperson	Decisional: entrepreneur, negotiator
Zeus: power-oriented, non-bureaucratic	✓		✗
Apollo: ordered/structured, rules and hierarchies		✓	✗
Athena: problem solving, teamwork	✗	✓	
Dionysus: individualism	✗		✓

- Interpersonal – where there is a clear need for a figurehead or leader

- Informational – where a monitoring and disseminating managerial style is required – effectively a spokesperson

- Decisional – when an entrepreneur is needed – someone who can handle disturbances and act as a negotiator

If we map these managerial approaches against Handy's management styles, the result is interesting (see Table 2.2).

This table suggests that it may not be easy to arrive at a happy marriage between style and required approach. A Zeus, for example, placed in an environment that demands a decisional and entrepreneurial approach to management, may struggle. If strong control is demanded, then having a Dionysus in charge is likely to be ineffective. If we then overlay these considerations with the suggestion that organizational structure may further compromise delivery against business objectives, we can see how much even general notions of 'management' can influence how organizational shape helps or hinders our ability to meet our objectives.

We might draw similar conclusions when considering leadership too. For many, management and leadership are one and the same thing; however people like John Adair (1934–) have argued that there is a real difference between managing and leading. For Adair, consideration of a team's performance suggests that 50% comes from 'self', and 50% from the way the team is led (see Boylan, 2001). Poor leadership can, therefore, severely compromise a team's ability to achieve 100% of its goals –

and for 'team' you can also read 'IT organization'. In these terms, what makes an effective leader? Perhaps, as Pearson (1992) suggests, it is more about personal attributes – such as drive, energy, vision, intelligence, mental and emotional health, and integrity – than about the way in which one goes about the job, i.e. the management style. A Dionysus-type manager placed in a decisional environment and working within a flat structure may seem an ideal combination; however, if the individual possesses little in the way of drive, energy, intelligence and so on, then their reign is likely to be less than successful.

On this basis, it might not be unreasonable of us to extend Adair's assertion and suggest that the overall success of the IT enterprise is dependent not only on self and leadership, but also on the managerial styles adopted allied with the approach needed. This could prove to be a highly complex matrix to draw out. If we overlay the implications of organizational structure onto this – either the defining of, or the impact from – we begin to get a sense of how complex this topic actually is; indeed, it is travelling ever further from a simplistic decision on hierarchical or flat structures.

2.1.4 Culture

The degree of success experienced in an IT organization may be governed by what is euphemistically termed 'culture'. For many, culture is something of an esoteric notion which can be easily discussed in generalities but which proves more difficult to actually define. People working within organizations talk about their culture – how good or bad it is, or how they have or need one – probably without being able to articulate exactly what they mean.

I would argue that there are worse ways of defining culture than by the combination of elements we have just been discussing, namely:

- The style of the overall manager (or, possibly, management team)
- The role the manager is required to play (interpersonal, informational, decisional)
- The quality of leadership (again for the overall manager or top team)
- Organizational shape

How it 'feels' to be working in a function will be largely defined by the combination of the above and how well the mix works. An Athena manager with poor leadership qualities, working within a non-matrix organizational structure yet in need of a decisional approach, is likely to generate a significant number of conflicts and points of failure within the function.

When considering the need for a 'change in culture', employees will most often point to a revision in one or more of the above to effect their desired goal; perhaps a new manager, a change in structure, a new vision, and so on. Also influencing this culture within the IT function will be the culture of the entire enterprise – which will, after all, be a macro (enterprise-level) combination of the above. In organizations with a very clear ethos and a well-understood culture, it is very often the Chief Executive who sets the tone and, most likely, achieves a balance between the various elements to minimize negative conflict: "the resilient organizational culture has a strong sense of enterprise purpose that cascades down and across the enterprise" (Bell, 2002).

How important is this general notion of culture? Day (2001) suggests that "a leadership model in which organizational design, the quality of team interactions, and the distribution of energy in the firm may be far more important determinants of success than the soundness of this or that strategy". The argument is that culture may be more important than strategy. A poor culture (the composite defined by me, above) has a limited chance of successfully implementing a strategy, no matter how good it is; a strong, positive culture can probably make a success of any strategy, even if it has some weaknesses.

2.1.5 A Generic Perspective

We need to be aware of these notions of management, leadership and culture if we are to shape our IT organization in such a way as to maximize its chance of being effective. This is not to say that there is any kind of slavish formula or analysis that must be followed in order to gain all appropriate foreknowledge. However, an IT manager who is aware of not only their own personal style, but also the demands upon them as to leadership needs and the management role they must play, will be assisted in influencing the organizational structure they put together. It is perhaps self-evident that this will still be primarily driven by their own style – Zeus, Apollo and so forth – but it is undoubtedly better to create a structure from a position of understanding all the challenges ahead.

There are many similar factors that can offer an influence at a secondary or tertiary level; some of these we will cover in Chapter 6. One that may

37

be worth considering at this point relates to a generic perspective about individuals – if only to remind ourselves that the perfect combination of our four culture components actually guarantees nothing, given that the delivery elements of our ideal organization remain individuals with their associated vagaries.

The work of Douglas McGregor (1906–64) led to a hypothesis in relation to a simplified categorization of people (see Boylan, 2001). McGregor's individuals were split into two camps:

- Theory X – the negative view of human behaviour, where people need to be appropriately driven and managed in order to achieve their goals
- Theory Y – the positive view, where people naturally seek fulfilment, and need less rigorous control to deliver as required

Whether one totally subscribes to McGregor's basic theory or not, it is certainly possible to see elements of both X and Y – to varying degrees – in those with whom we interact on a daily basis. For a manager putting together his organization (both in terms of the naked structure and then filling that structure with appropriate resources) an appreciation of his staff at this most basic of levels can pay dividends. For example, a role may exist for an individual with a particular mix of technical skills to lead a virtual team on a Research and Development project. Of two candidates, Ben is clearly better technically; but the manager knows this person to be an X-type, unlike Max who, though technically slightly weaker, is much more self-reliant and self-starting. Who should he appoint? Probably Max. Without knowing Ben and Max well enough as people, Ben would be the clear choice. If Ben were chosen then it is still possible that man-managing him tightly could mitigate against the inefficient functions likely to result from this appointment, but this effectively results in additional overhead. The manager would need to be aware of this and plan/structure accordingly.

This is not such a far-fetched example. One might argue that managers fall broadly into two categories: the 'hands-off' and the 'hands-on'. If the former, the manager needs to be supported by Y-types whose styles also possess sufficient control and monitoring. Surrounding themselves with direct reports who were innovative Y-types but not process conscious would probably lead to a very loose and essentially ill-disciplined organization. One could draw similar examples of bad matches for the hands-on manager. Whatever the mix, the manager should also be aware of the 'lowest common denominator' factor, i.e. it is entirely possible that having one or more X-types within a group of people could potentially act as a drag on the overall team, and result in putting in place methods of management and control that had a negative effect on the majority of the team.

In concluding this particular section, I hope I have illustrated that there are a number of factors – mainly around individual styles, approaches and so on – to suggest that putting together a well-structured and effective IT organization is not simply about the shape of boxes on an organogram. As much as anything else it is about the people we choose to fill those boxes and the roles we ask them to play.

2.2 Organizational Components in IT

2.2.1 Operations

Having now considered some generic theoretical components in relation to organizational structure, it is prudent at this point to ensure that we have a suitable datum for the IT function in particular. After all, if we are going on to debate the format and shape of individual elements within the IT structure, we need to ensure that we have a common understanding of the blocks with which we are building – if only to abide by a consistency of terminology.

Take the Operations function for example. This is likely to be the most common element across all IT functions, yet may not be immediately recognizable to some through the name I have chosen to apply to it. So what do I mean by 'Operations'? In defining the general IT functions with which we will be concerned, I propose to firstly suggest some of the broad responsibilities within each area and then highlight some of the key elements or potential issues associated with the section from an organizational perspective. We will discuss potential future models for these functions later.

So when I talk about 'Operations' what do I mean? This is the unit whose responsibility is to maintain the well-being of the systems infrastructure for which the IT department is responsible. On this basis, things such as:

● Hardware maintenance and servicing (including personal computers)

● Capacity planning

- Network and communications infrastructure (including external connections)

- Operating system(s) maintenance, patching and upgrading

- Security

- Database management

- Some applications maintenance

Thus, the Operations function is critical to the day-to-day operation and maintenance of the overall systems environment. They do not – in the main – deliver any form of business-led change, however; change introduced by the Operations teams will, more often than not, remain invisible to the end user.

From an organizational perspective, we should consider the following influencing items:

- There will need to be an emphasis on controls and well-documented and managed procedures.

- Solid change control processes will be needed.

- Escalations paths should be clearly defined.

- Service-level agreements may be in force.

- Interaction with the end user base is likely to be limited.

- Operation is likely to be required $24 \times 7 \times 365$ (in some form or another).

- Appropriate hand-offs with other areas of the IT function will need to be in place (something that should be a default for all subfunctions).

Although not our primary concern at this point, it is worthwhile noting how even drawing up a simple list such as this can begin to help us define the kind of organization – and people – required for Operations to be successful. We can, for example, ask ourselves what kind of manager sits better at the top of such a department, a Dionysus or a Zeus? What kind of management style is likely to be required, informational or interpersonal? How might we be affected here in terms of the X- or Y-theory people balance? I suggest that such things are rarely considered.

2.2.2 Help Desk

Most commonly the help desk is a group of people who reside within the overall Operations area, given that their responsibility is, to some degree, the maintenance of the existing infrastructure (as we shall see). However, I have decided to recognize the help desk as a separate entity for the purposes of this argument, primarily on the basis that there are some additional areas of responsibility that quite obviously sets them apart.

So when we talk about the help desk, to what should we be referring?

- First point of call for Users/Customers with issues, questions, etc.
- Problem resolution for desktop-related productivity tools (e.g. acting as the first line telephone fix for queries around software such as the Microsoft Office suite)
- Problem ownership for issues which need to be resolved elsewhere (e.g. in Operations or Application Development)
- Systems administration functions (e.g. password control)
- Focal point for globally visible issues such as virus alerts and control

This list can be extended (or contracted), depending on the size of the overall enterprise and the IT function in particular. For example, in very large international companies the help desk is likely to remain physically remote from a large proportion of its user community, with interaction being almost entirely telephone-based. In smaller businesses, the help desk may also have the responsibility of physically visiting an individual machine (usually a PC) to effect call resolution in a hands-on manner (second-line fix).

Some of the organizational imperatives around the help desk function will be very similar to those already suggested for the Operations function; significantly, however, some will not:

- There will need to be some emphasis on controls and documented procedures.
- Change control processes will be needed (where appropriate).
- Escalation paths should be clearly defined.
- Service level agreements may be in force.

- Service may be required $24 \times 7 \times 365$ (though only in very large, perhaps multi-national organizations).

- Interaction with the end user base is a significant part of the job.

- Individuals taking ownership of issues is key.

- Personal characteristics (being helpful, positive, friendly, etc.) are likely to be as important as technical skills.

The last three points are one of the key reasons for recognizing that there may be some merit in pulling the help desk out of Operations to assist with our analysis. For example, the suggestions we might chose to make for the 'culture' of Operations (based on our four key components) will almost certainly not prove to be the best fit for a function such as the help desk where the culture must, by definition, be different.

2.2.3 Applications Development

In tackling the 'change' area of the systems function – as against the operational or service areas already considered – I intend to take a similar approach. Namely, in addressing the subject of Applications Development, I am going to separate out 'Business Engagement' and 'Project Management' on the basis that these – like the help desk – have discrete attributes that will benefit from explicit consideration. If we are to be successful in moving forwards in our attempts to define the 'best fit' IT organization for any given situation, then we should not risk losing critical front-line departmental functions or roles by attempting to submerge them into one large pot.

Of course the Applications Development area, even without engagement and project management aspects, is still a significant beast. Change can be delivered in anything from a simple PC database through to an enterprise-wide ERP or CRM (Customer Relationship Management) system. Despite this breadth, there will be a core number of responsibilities residing here:

- Delivery of software (business applications and associated processes) to effect some form of business change or operational enhancement

- Definition and agreement of business requirements

- Definition of systems needs based on defined business requirements

- Development, configuration or amendment of appropriate tools or packages to manufacture applications based on the given requirements

- Testing developed applications as 'fit for purpose' (quality control)

- Delivery of new or amended applications into a 'live' or production environment

- Support of live applications to maintain their 'fit for purpose' status

In environments where some of this work is contracted out, in addition to all of these still being valid there are extra management responsibilities with respect to the supplier of the development service. I intend to cover these under a broad definition of Business Engagement. Of course, we are going on to consider outsourcing in a little more detail later; for the moment perhaps we should just note that however we approach the organization of our own function in this area, we are likely to have more limited influence over the parallel activity in the supplier's business.

Our definition of Application Development focuses very much on the delivery aspects of the work undertaken: delivery of a definition of the requirements; the systems interpretation of those requirements; building and testing the solution; then in-life support. In many respects this pattern fits a general manufacturing and product management model. Organizationally there are many different opinions as to the ways in which the application environment can bet set up. Leaving this aside for the moment – and keeping in mind that we are talking about a form of manufacturing and product management model – then we might reasonably point to the following as being key factors in our definition of structure:

- There will need to be some emphasis on controls and documented procedures with respect to development approach.

- Change control processes will be needed (for applications both in-life and in development).

- Development is unlikely to be required $24 \times 7 \times 365$, although some provision for out-of-hours application support will probably be needed.

- Interaction with the end user base is likely to be a significant part of the job for a proportion of the function.

- Individuals will need to take ownership of the elements of the development or application for which they have responsibility.

- The function is likely to need a mix of positive personal characteristics and technical skills, depending on the role to be carried out.

- There will need to be a testing function (allied to quality control).

As we can immediately see, this portfolio is far more broad than that suggested for the operational areas of the IT function. The range of skills, styles and expertise required will vary considerably between 'front' and 'back' functions such as Business Analysts and Testers. For this reason it is harder to offer any immediate generalizations as to the need for a particular combination or culture which will fit the applications area exactly. We will return to this particular conundrum later.

2.2.4 Business Engagement

So where is the boundary between Business Engagement and Application Development? Indeed, we have already suggested in the section above that part of the remit of the applications function is the definition of business requirements, and what is this if not engagement with the business? For my part, I intend to classify this analysis activity as very much part of the manufacturing process. The engagement I now have in mind is that which is abstracted one level further up the IT food chain, i.e. with those managers and executives from whom support and funding for projects and programmes is needed, and with whom systems, strategies and priorities to drive the future direction of the IT function are agreed.

In many organizations such activity is an adjunct to the role of the project manager, if recognized at all. Where there is a tendency to work on a project-by-project basis, then the engagement that takes place at this level can often bypass anything that smacks of setting overall strategies and priorities. However, given the changing business environment to which we have already alluded, it seems reasonable to suggest that only through co-operative business-led objective setting can we really be certain that the direction IT is taking is the most appropriate.

Of course our new engagement models must also include businesses outside of the local parent. In adopting outsourcing strategies a new set of engagement demands are thrown in the IT manager's direction; and the recognition of IT-specific interfaces with suppliers' and customers' own operations also suggests that we need to approach the general engagement subject in a less piecemeal fashion. Thus I would argue that for business engagement we are looking at:

- Working with the internal User community to define high-level business-driven IT strategies

- Working with the internal User community to prioritize and monitor IT projects and programmes based on business demand

- Acting in a consultative fashion to assist the business in solving commercial problems and challenges

- Actively managing outsourcing IT arrangements on behalf of the business

- Working collaboratively with suppliers and customers on e-business systems initiatives

- Generally representing the IT function on behalf of the enterprise

It is obvious that there are a mix of skills and organizational imperatives here that would not sit so well in our manufacturing development function. Of course, operations will have some of the kinds of supplier contact referred to above, and deciding where the responsibility for this kind of relationship management lies will be one of the many subtleties of putting together any IT structure.

So what are the key organizational nuances to be taken from the business engagement area?

- There will be a relatively limited need for controls and documented procedures (except in the area of SLA management with outsourcing suppliers).

- Fundamentally engagement is likely to be a 'core hours' activity.

- Interaction with those outside of the function is the raison d'être for this area.

- Individuals need to take ownership of relationships rather than systems, applications or technologies.

- The function will demand a certain range of personal characteristics as core competencies for the job.

Once again, even with a simple list such as this, we can see that the kinds of individuals who would thrive amongst these challenges might be hard pressed to contribute effectively in some of the other IT subfunctions already examined. Business engagement, if it is to be done well and done effectively, needs a particular type of animal – supported by a set of cultural values appropriate to the role.

2.2.5 Project Management

The final substantial subfunction that I wish to consider here is that of Project Management. A little like business engagement, project management is often seen as part of the applications development process where individuals, related by specific knowledge of particular technologies, have enough of a skill-set or bent to be able to undertake a task-oriented management role. However, we should be clear that project management is as distinct an undertaking as engagement.

In addition to the uniqueness of the make-up of those who go to make good project managers, there are a number of other reasons why distinction is merited. We have already seen, for example, how more and more projects are likely to expand beyond the domestic function and user base. Particularly in the area of collaborative e-business initiatives there may be a fundamental need for 'integrated' project management, that is where individual managers looking after discrete and local projects need to come together to contribute to the management of the collective initiative. In these circumstances project managers need to be more than part-time or part-skilled. The picture is similar in situations where outsourcing agencies are responsible for the delivery of a particular project (which could, remember, be in the operations area as much as in applications). These projects will need good quality project management to ensure the best chance of success.

The brief of project managers must therefore include things such as:

- Project planning skills (including budgetary planning)
- Emphasis on controls and documented procedures with respect to project tracking and reporting
- Man-management skills at the task allocation level
- An understanding of risk and issue management
- Change control processes will be needed in relation to project plans

- Interaction with end users (or external agencies) is likely to be an important part of the job

- Individuals will need to take responsibility for the delivery of the entire project in accordance with the agreed schedules and budgets

- The role is likely to need a mix of appropriate personal characteristics (for example to ensure credibility with project sponsors) and technical skills

This mix is somewhat different again from those to which we have already alluded. More and more, organizations are coming to recognize that project management is a discipline rather than a skill, and explicit demands from employers for demonstration of this discipline (through recognized accreditation) are growing. In many companies project managers are being removed from any kind of line management role based around an application or technology and are being grouped in their own dedicated 'pool' for utilization across the whole IT spectrum.

For project managers to be organizationally effective, we need to recognize:

- There will need to be considerable emphasis on controls and documented procedures.

- Fundamentally this is likely to be a 'core hours' activity.

- Interaction will be with those both inside and outside the project area.

- Individuals will need to take ownership of projects and a variable mix of relationships, systems, applications and technologies (at the project level).

- The function will demand a defined range of personal characteristics as core competencies for the job.

- Change control processes will be needed (where appropriate).

- Management reporting and escalation paths should be clearly defined.

- The resources can be co-located with other subfunctions or as a discrete pool (they may also sit in a 'grey' area between IT and the business).

If one also considers the particular demands on project managers in setting up, managing and maintaining project-related organisms such as

Table 2.3. 'Cultural' Mix of IT Subfunctions

	Management style				Management approach			Structure			
	Zeus	Apollo	Athena	Dionysus	Interpersonal	Informational	Decisional	Hierarchical	Flat	Matrix	Support
Operations	✓					✓		✓			
Help Desk		✓				✓					✓
Applications Development			✓				✓			✓	
Business Engagement				✓	✓				✓		
Project Management		✓					✓		✓		

steering groups or project boards, it is clear that we can argue that the entire combination differentiates itself from the other groupings we have thus far considered.

In order to illustrate this point (albeit in a somewhat crude fashion) Table 2.3 offers a suggested view of the five subfunctions we have just discussed against some of our core culture criteria.

Whilst not an exhaustive analysis, this generalized position does indeed show how such functions differ – and how we need to take these differences into account if we are going to ensure effective organizational planning.

2.2.6 The Silo Tendency

Before leaving this section on the organizational components of the IT function, there are two general and related issues which we need to discuss. These are not, perhaps, unique to IT (as opposed to any other department within an organization), however they do have the capability to derail any endeavour aimed at organizational change.

The first of these I have termed the 'silo tendency'. By this I mean the inclination for subfunctions within an IT organization to concentrate entirely on themselves when it comes to how they are comprised and act, how they define the culture by which they operate, and so on. Thus, the operations function may see itself as being clearly separate from applications or project management, and move forward on that basis. As Foote et al. (2001) suggest, "these units have their own business plans, resources, channels, and customer relationships; status and power bases are built on the units and their products". Whilst this comment may have been aimed at larger entities, it can still apply to our subfunctions within IT. For example, there may be a number of groups within IT who need to engage with a particular business unit. If they pursue these engagements in a blinkered fashion, a number of things can arise:

- The customer has too many interfaces into IT.

- Duplication of roles can be created across the IT department.

- In areas such as engagement or project management, IT is likely both to be less effective and to fail to reap the benefits from a number of internal synergies, e.g. cross-silo knowledge transfer.

Such a tendency can have a significantly negative effect on the final shape of the IT organization if it is allowed not only to exist but also to prevail. Given some of the business drivers that are effectively being transferred into IT, one can argue that it is important that a holistic view of the systems organization is taken. Of course this becomes even more difficult if the current function is set solid. It is surely true that "radical change is difficult in established organizational units" (Nyström, 1996), and if radical change is required to effect the appropriate organizational changes needed, then internal IT silos will only get in the way.

2.2.7 The Introspective Tendency

The second observation is a tendency towards introspection. By that I mean that when the IT function is planning or preparing for a change to its internal organization, very often it will draw the blinds around itself and pursue an entirely self-absorbed focus. In many respects this is the silo mentality writ large. There are both inherent and implied dangers in this.

The inherent danger is that in the pursuit of a new 'ideal' model, the IT department will ignore not only the demands being placed upon it by the business but also the way in which the business itself is structured. The potential problem here is clear. When the IT manager takes the wraps off his new organization he may find that it is poorly aligned to the rest of the business – thereby making the key task of engagement more difficult – and is not best structured to deliver against known commercial priorities and goals – thereby almost 'building in' failure. By its very nature reorganizing has to be an 'internal' exercise, but it should not be wholly so.

One way to mitigate against this is to canvass opinions from outside of IT in order to understand exactly what is expected by the function's customers and to recognize where current failings may exist. After all, it is perfectly possible to believe that a certain aspect of the organization is failing when in fact customer perception indicates the complete reverse. If at all possible, one should endeavour to follow the old maxim, 'if it isn't broken, don't fix it'.

The implied danger in this introspective tendency comes at the corporate level; namely where one or more functions outside of IT reorganizes itself without reference to any other. For the systems community this can mean that solid working relationships and processes are unnecessarily broken; that there is suddenly an expectation for IT to work in a completely different way; that new business demands (which drove the reorganization in Product Management, for example) are sprung on an IT function that now cannot meet them.

It is obvious that these kinds of challenges are political ones that need to be recognized at the level of corporate culture. By illustrating them, however, it does help us to demonstrate that reshaping an organization is most definitely a two-way street, and that the effects of a disastrous change will be felt outside the function too.

2.3 Organization Life Cycle

2.3.1 Recognizing the Atrophy Model

There are undoubtedly many people who are unsettled by change and overly influenced by the negative connotations it can bring with it. Perhaps this is particularly so in a function where – despite the fact that IT is essentially about enabling change – one might wish to argue that delivering a successful systems product is dependent upon providing an environment which is stable and managed by well-defined and known processes. There is, of course, much to be said for this argument. If one is aiming to improve quality standards, for example, this could be made considerably harder by continually changing build processes in the 'manufacturing' environment. The argument against change fails to recognize two things, however. The first of these comes in the shape of the new business drivers which, by their very nature of being more rapid, fluid and dynamic than ever before, cascade a need for almost continual change into the IT function. The second lies in the nature of organizations themselves.

Sturges and Brewerton (2002) have argued that patterns of reliability in engineering can be adapted to fit an organizational model. For example, when we buy a new car we can be certain that at some point in the future we will need to replace the tyres, the oil, the brake pads, and so on. They simply wear out. When we need to do so will depend upon a number factors, of course: how far and how fast we drive being key. Furthermore, whether these elements will need to be replaced systematically, coincidentally, or piecemeal may be partly down to chance; some we can fit within planned maintenance, others will just happen – a nail in a tyre, for example.

The argument follows that all organizations have a limited life span too. There is a 'natural cycle' of organizational development, maturity and decay, and that at the end of the cycle something needs to happen to prevent collapse and failure.

Figure 2.1 depicts this pattern. Following a period of development where the organization is defined, where new people are appointed and roles clarified, the structure settles down into its period of maturity. It begins to operate 'naturally', i.e. the organizational dynamics – such as 'culture' – take over and the structure simply 'functions'. (It is important to note here that the way the organization behaves may prove not to be along the lines intended. Once the structure is established it must take on a life of its own, driven by the needs, agendas, strengths and fallibilities of those individuals working within it.)

At some point, the organization will begin to function less well. Why might this be the case? Perhaps there are some key resources that leave the company, thereby changing skill-sets, culture and dynamics. In IT terms, there will be a continual stream of influences coming from outside the department, where new business initiatives – such as e-business – demand different ways of delivery. Whatever the cause, at some point organizational atrophy will set in.

As Sturges and Brewerton (2002) point out, "the goal of management is to achieve a state where people and technology make maximum contribution to the organization's accomplishment of its objectives with

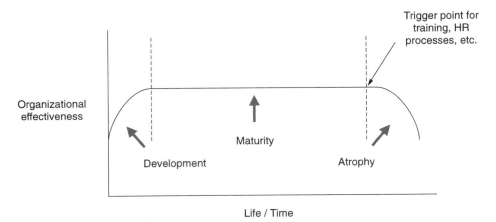

Figure 2.1. *Organizational Life Cycle*

minimum probability of failure of any specific organizational component". In effect, this means that on our atrophy model the 'maturity' line should be as high up the graph as possible (maximizing objectives) and there for as long as possible (minimizing failure). Essentially the objective is organizational effectiveness, i.e. getting it 'right'.

2.3.2 The Impact of Doing Nothing

It is entirely possible that one might choose to dismiss the atrophy argument perhaps on the grounds that when structural change comes it is usually driven from higher up the enterprise and that the IT department is often 'done to', i.e. it is outside of local control. If this were the case, then I would argue that we have an example of external influence triggering the next development cycle.

Perhaps one might fail to recognize that, whatever it may be called, changes in local structures actually fit the atrophy model; in this case I suspect that after a very limited amount of study one could effectively prove that it is most likely they do. Or perhaps one might choose to suggest that the entire function is in such a constant state of flux that it never leaves the 'development' phase. To counter this, we might suggest that this is a symptom of the maturity phase being incredibly short – and the organizational shape being 'wrong' in the first place.

Whichever view we possess, I would argue that there is no excuse for doing nothing. The atrophy argument seems to me to be a sound premiss that, as a generic theory, fits the cyclical development of the IT organization very well. Indeed, accepting it as such provides us with a useful template in terms of organizational planning. Of course one of the prerequisites of this working is our being able to identify the critical point on the curve, i.e. when we are making the transition from maturity to decay.

In order to achieve this, there will need to be a means of measuring the performance of the function as a whole. The use of metrics within IT is nothing new, and those that measure things such as system downtime, budget and timescale performance, productivity and so on – and which should already be in place – can prove the most useful. They are, after all, measures of organizational effectiveness, and the IT manager would want to see them move positively after the introduction of a structural change. Throughout the period of maturity, the aim should be to see at worst a level trend in terms of performance, though a slight increase would be ideal. It is when these trends turn towards the negative that one would get the first warning signs.

In Figure 2.1 I have suggested that at this point a number of HR-related activities might be undertaken: additional training, bonus incentives, and so forth. These are aimed at people as individuals rather than the structure as a whole. As such they may help to reverse the decline – particularly if the reversal is no more than a 'blip', which it might be – but will do nothing significant if the issue is that the shape of the organization no longer fits the demands being placed upon it.

It is in these circumstances that doing nothing ceases to be an option for the IT manager. If the structure of the function becomes fundamentally flawed then they will be faced with an ever-downward trend in terms of measured performance. Other attributes of the organization are likely to suffer too: perhaps the attrition rate begins to rise and morale begins to fall; perhaps IT's reputation begins to decline with more negative comment coming from the department's customers. Under such conditions doing nothing fails to recognize the imperative of the atrophy model. Once in decline the structure of the function must be reviewed.

2.3.3 Implications in an IT Environment

In asserting the atrophy model and applying it to the structure of an IT organization, my premiss is that when we have evidence of a decline in effectiveness we need to act and review the overall function. I am less concerned with the triggers that may have generated this recognition. We have already suggested a number of these:

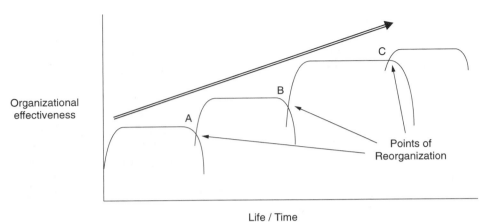

Figure 2.2. Organizational Development

- Restructuring drivers at the corporate level (not strictly atrophy based, though restructures in customer departments may well indicate that the IT function is about to fall into decline, e.g. alignment and engagement models may cease to be appropriate)

- Business demands require the IT function to deliver different things, attack new technologies, meet challenges around shortened timescales; in these cases the atrophy effects are likely to be cumulative

- Where there is real internal atrophy; for example, through the loss of key resources, or where particular 'cultural' mixes are failing to deliver

The potential result is shown in Figure 2.2.

Here we have an example of an IT function which, after establishing its initial structural model, goes through three cycles of reshaping. As suggested in the diagram, these organizational changes will not necessarily be uniform. The 'depth' of the curve on the graph suggests the degree of change in terms of how sweeping or radical it is, and perhaps how much of the function is affected. The length of the maturity element shows how long any structure remains effective. Thus we can see that change 'B' appears more wholesale and radical than the reshaping that occurred before it. On the other hand, change 'C' – in being relatively shallow – represents what may be a minor adjustment to the structure extant at that time.

You might look at such a representation with horror if you infer that I am arguing for nothing but constant flux. However, we need to remember that the x-axis is time and that the span represented in Figure 2.2 could be anything from two years to perhaps ten years. In these cases the atrophy theory obviously does not indicate a life of constant change within the IT community.

There is one final point to be taken from this argument. As I have suggested in Figure 2.2, the cumulative effect of our organizational changes is to improve the effectiveness of the entire function over time. Indeed, apart from addressing situations where there are explicit failures in the function, why else would we want to change organizational structures if it is not to improve the products delivered? Measures can, as referred to earlier, prove such increases in performance – and once proven, can provide a useful tool in getting business support for future changes if this is needed. On this basis – and in conclusion – the atrophy model of organizational change is in no way negative. It is a mechanism that allows the recognition of a very real phenomenon, and which can be turned into a tool for driving consistent and long-term business benefit.

Why Change?

3

3.1 Introduction

3.1.1 So What?

Thus far I have attempted to define the issues facing the IT community in terms of its organizational shape and how this relates not only to the business pressures it confronts but also in terms of the life of the organization itself. We have outlined the kind of problems the function must address and the key considerations for IT from a 'commercial' perspective, e.g. the implications of e-business and the need to provide good value-for-money and sound ROI. In addition, we have discussed a number of generic topics around organizational shape, such as flat vs. hierarchical organizations and the nature and composition of 'culture'. These we related back to specific subfunctions within the IT structure to illustrate the subtleties of organizational design as faced by the IT manager. Finally, at the end of Chapter 2, we discussed the theory of organizational atrophy, how this argument supports the need for change and revision of the IT structure over time, and how these remodelling exercises could also work towards long-term improvement of functional efficiency and performance.

It is possible that there will be some who, having reached this point, remain unconvinced. The position that 'things have worked OK thus far, so why do I need to accept these arguments?' may still be believed to be tenable even though the landscape of 'things have worked OK thus far' will have almost certainly included past organizational reshapings that actually comply with our atrophy model.

Therefore in this chapter I intend to delve a little deeper into some of the topics already introduced in order to demonstrate that there are benefits to be gained from considering IT organizational shape from a new and more thorough perspective. In evaluating some of our recognized drivers, we will begin to consider exactly how IT can mould itself to best deliver against these. To this end, we will cover the following:

- Addressing business demand and commercial pressures, including the organizational response to issues such as the demand for efficiency, the broader skills spectrum and demise of staff loyalty

- Opportunity drivers and the need for continuous improvement, including the impact of technological change

- How IT can be organized to ensure a tie-in with its customers when it comes to overall business objectives

- Portfolio management as a tool for the IT function – and the organization needed to support it

- The organizational issues around the customer 'front end', and issues and options in the engagement space

Finally in this chapter we will consider disaggregation as a potential organizational template for the modern IT function, and the kinds of business alignment models that might be adopted in support of this.

3.1.2 Addressing Business Demand and Commercial Pressures

There can be no doubt that we are now experiencing one of the most turbulent periods ever seen in times of 'normal' business activity, i.e. not driven by some general catastrophe, economic meltdown, or war. Not only do we see new technology pushing radical initiatives and fresh business models, but also enterprises are in the merger phase of the 'big is beautiful/small is beautiful' cycle. Research from the Gartner Group (quoted by Mahoney, 2001) suggests that "90 percent of enterprises have undertaken a major change affecting at least half their overall organization in the last two years". Taken literally this means that of the working population, only one in ten will be on the payroll of a company that was organizationally the same at the beginning of 2002 as it was at the beginning of 2000; and that around 50% of the entire corporate workforce will have been directly affected by some organizational change or another.

These are massive numbers. Of course the research does not suggest that all these changes directly include the IT functions of the enterprises concerned – but even if they do not, IT will have been impacted through explicit changes in structures elsewhere and the knock-on effects in

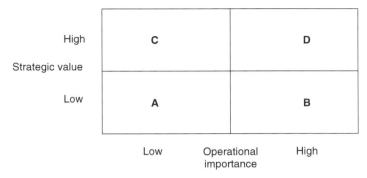

Figure 3.1. Strategic Value vs. Operational Importance

terms of engagement models, business channels, product strategies and so forth. If Gartner's figure is not staggering enough, it is probably also true that each of us as consumers have had dealings with at least one of the companies which has undergone such changes, i.e. potentially all consumers are dealing with a 'transformed' company.

These are serious enough drivers to suggest that the IT function – from an organizational perspective – must keep pace with the general corporate community. Additionally, when businesses are being restructured they will be looking at a whole mix of areas from the perspective of value-for-money and ROI: exactly those same areas of focus from which IT is likely to be scrutinized. Take a merger between two companies, for example. Without considering the explicit implications on the IT departments, it is entirely likely that studies will be undertaken to identify where greatest business benefit can be gained, perhaps in defining the new product portfolio. In this instance, it is entirely possible that products may be categorized along similar lines to the Boston matrix (Barton, 2002) shown in Chapter 1 (and repeated here as Figure 3.1). Even customers can be analysed in this way.

Once the commercial analysis has been carried out and the products which reside in the critical 'boxes' defined (likely to be 'B', 'C' and 'D') there may be a knock-on effect in the IT function when the business demands that systems and resource focus on 'D' as a priority, with 'B' and 'C' as secondary importance. Systems and resources focused in supporting the products which reside in 'A' may need to be withdrawn altogether. Responding to such business demands by simply 'shuffling the pack' and shifting resources supporting the 'A' products into existing structures whose output is vaguely aimed at the other quadrants, is

59

simply not enough. The business has issued a new strategic plan and one to which IT – and the IT organization – must be acutely aligned.

Of course one of the prime business objectives in recent times is cost cutting. Mergers and acquisitions are often undertaken with the objective of getting 100% of the combined product and/or customer base, but with only 80% of the resource. Under cost-cutting scenarios (and we will consider outsourcing explicitly later on) very often the IT community is seen as a ripe target. The IT manager might be asked to lose 20% of his staff or reduce his budget by 15% and so on. Under these circumstances, the temptation might be to maintain an existing structure which may be working well and reduce each ten-man team by two.

However, as the Meta Group (2002) point out, "indiscriminate cost cutting can result in an organization becoming too heavily invested in technologies that are not essential to the business, while starving core necessities". Thus, not only may the ability to deliver critical systems be impacted, the function may be striving to keep alive applications and technologies that it might do better to drop altogether. As with the newly combined product set, a cost-cutting initiative is a revised corporate strategy, and IT must look to its organizational shape in the light of this if it is to ensure the maintenance of maximum effectiveness, value for money and ROI.

3.1.3 'Do more with less'

Cost-cutting directives are perhaps the most obvious methods to be employed by the 'do more with less' mentality that strives for ultra-competitive, lean-and-mean enterprises. But it would be wrong of us to think that, from the IT perspective, this is simply about cutting headcount and budget. As I have suggested above, a reduction in staff numbers may mean that the structure of the function needs to be revisited. Whilst this will inevitably be seen as a negative initiative, there may be some opportunities too.

Given that the business is in a belt-tightening scenario, corporate managers should look to IT not only to cut its own costs, but also to assist the rest of the business in reducing theirs. This is something other than adoption of new commercial models. As Beck (2002) suggests, "technology assets must be applied to business goals for operational efficiencies, as well as for business transformation". Thus, given a solid business case, there may actually be an argument for *introducing* new technologies to enable the 'do more with less' mentality across the business – and if this applies to technologies, then it must surely apply to the people who manage it.

Take a crude example. An IT function can group its systems into the quadrants of the Boston matrix (Figure 3.1). In each segment, there are 25 people building, delivering and supporting the systems in one way or another. The IT manager is told to cut his workforce by 20%, i.e. down to 80. As we have already suggested, reducing the number of resources in each quadrant to 20 would be the simplest, most obvious and least correct approach. In looking at the challenge he faces, the IT manager identifies that by implementing a new Knowledge Management (KM) system he can assist the Customer Services function to reduce its headcount without loss of service, as well as offer significant improvements elsewhere; people will gain a broader knowledge base and the enterprise can effectively do as much with fewer individuals. The project, which requires five people, is approved; but now it appears as if the IT manager needs to reduce from 105 to 80 people. When he now looks at his structure he has something positive to add to the mix (which helps morale), and his remodelled function may end up looking like 30 people supporting systems in 'D' (including the five to cater for the new KM system), 20 people in each of 'B' and 'C', and 10 in 'A'. In this way he hits his target, provides maximum focus to both business objectives and critical systems, and can constructively decommission those systems that provide least value or ROI to the business (those in quadrant 'A'). He could only do this by recognizing the impact of the new corporate strategy and realigning organizationally to fit.

Exactly how that new organization looks from a structural perspective may change too. There may have been a strictly hierarchical framework in place previously, but in order to hit the resource target he has been set, the IT manager may choose to adopt something slightly more flexible to ensure that some people can work across teams, i.e. move to a matrix structure in some areas. It may also be that the KM system can only be delivered in conjunction with some third parties. Here, a change to something 'relational' may be called for: a structure that recognizes the need to work in partnership with a group outside the company. For Day and Wendler (1998) "'relational' forms of organization … include alliances, joint ventures, long-term supplier relationships, and licensing arrangements". Thus it is not just the numbers or where they are focused that may be changed in the 'do more with less' scenario; there may be a need to change the underlying shape of the organization – both in terms of structure and type of structure – if the IT manager is to remain successful.

3.1.4 The Broader Skills Spectrum

Defining what people do – and what they are expected to do – is another reason for the IT manager to adopt a different approach towards the strategy for his organization. Indeed, in the simple example quoted in the previous section we hinted as much when referring to the need for matrix or relational structures.

In IT organizational models from the recent past, structures would have been relatively simple; they would usually be strictly hierarchical (to various degrees of depth), and individuals would have been shown along with their job title. Thus Mike is a Team Leader, David an Analyst, and Fred a Programmer; within their team structure both David and Fred report to Mike, who in turn reports to the IT manager. Across the applications function there are a number of teams that mirror this formation. The job titles describe exactly what these three people do: Mike leads the Team and no longer performs any of the functions of an Analyst; David has been promoted, aspires to team leadership and no longer writes computer software; and so on. However, as technology has become more sophisticated it has begun to blur role delineations within the manufacturing element of the IT function. Now the tools that Fred uses to write programs effectively force him into the space nominally reserved for David; as a result, David is finding his monopoly on analytical skills being challenged. The good news for David, however, is that as his skills are not technology specific, he can assist other teams by offering his expertise there.

This should not be an unfamiliar scenario. Indeed, this blurring and migration of skills and job roles has led to a number of structural notions which clearly challenge the simple hierarchical model:

- 'Dotted-line reporting' – in our example above, where David now also reports to Tom, another Team Leader on whose project he is also working

- 'Virtual teams' – it may be that Tom has no dedicated resource of his own, and he delivers his project entirely through dotted-line reports

- 'Resource pools' – where David may be taken out of Mike's team altogether and placed in a pool of analyst resources who work on projects as and when required, potentially more than one at a time

None of these notions are new to us, but what we may not have recognized is that in many instances they are driven by – and a symptom of –

the broadening of skill-sets within the IT function. The Mike, David and Fred example is a simple illustration as to how dotted-line reporting, virtual teams and resource pools can come about. Indeed, I could have chosen many other examples.

The key for us here is not only to recognize the trend (and perhaps what has caused it or what drives it on), but also to acknowledge that it forces us to look at the shape of the IT organization in a different way. It is another element which must push us away from our traditional views on organizational design, and which challenges our structural thinking.

3.1.5 Wither Loyalty?

Finally, a word on staff mobility. The shift in technological sophistication has, as we have seen above, led to a number of new concepts and structures within the IT organization. It has also driven a significant increase in mobility – and an associated decrease in company loyalty. What do I mean by this?

Perhaps as recently as ten or fifteen years ago, the range of skills that an IT professional could aspire to have was relatively limited. There were generic roles – such as Operator, Programmer, and so on – and within these a defined list of technology-focused specialisms – COBOL, IBM MVS, CICS, etc. However, the burgeoning software and network-based operating systems market has significantly changed this. For example, from the days where finance or warehousing systems were written in-house using COBOL programmers, we now have new concepts in software applications around Enterprise Resource Planning (ERP) and Customer Relationship Management (CRM). Not only that, but these markets are further sub-divided by the specific applications themselves. Crudely speaking, we have moved from having one hundred 'generic' COBOL programmers, to having ten J.D.Edwards specialists, ten SAP specialists, ten Siebel specialists, and so on.

Utilizing simple economics, we can see that this does a number of things: firstly, it creates pools of scarce resource (the specialists); secondly, the scarcity increases the cost of those resources; thirdly, not only do individuals become more critical, they are also more likely to be lured away. This is far removed from scenarios where COBOL programmers were pretty much interchangeable.

This increase in the fluidity or dynamic of the resource pool has structural implications for the IT manager. Traditional IT organization

63

models were developed when there was less fluidity and greater loyalty, when individuals were not 'key', and when more people stayed in the same company for a significant number of years. Now the IT manager must be able to respond to individual departures in a much more aggressive way than before if he is to ensure that disproportionate damage is not done to his delivery capability. Organizationally this means that his structure must be able to accommodate flexibility to enable response to losing key individuals – and that he should recognize the importance of those people in the first place and undertake contingency or succession planning. Fifteen years ago neither of these would have been relevant considerations in the vast majority of cases.

3.2 Opportunity-driven Change

3.2.1 The Need for Continuous Improvement

In addition to the challenges facing the IT organization as outlined in the previous section, there are other more positive opportunities which, if they are to be taken by the systems community, also imply the need for a revised way of looking at the structure. Indeed, without undertaking a refreshed view, the IT manager may find himself incapable of rising to these challenges and reaping the associated benefits. There is a generic argument too. By tailoring the IT function in such a way as to maximize its ability to seize opportunities that come its way, we can potentially create a virtuous circle. Eisenstat et al. (2001) suggest that "opportunity-based organizations … look for a richer variety of opportunities"; if this is true, then an IT function that has a proven capability to be successful in this space may find itself with increased support from the business community when suggesting new initiatives.

In one of our earlier examples we talked about the implementation of a Knowledge Management system whilst in the middle of resource downsizing. Being able to undertake this project would, in a large part, be driven by the capability of the IT function to take it on from an organizational perspective. If this implementation is successful, when the IT manager then suggests adopting new Content Management technologies to achieve the same effect, the business is more likely to listen to and support him.

Some opportunities are, somewhat paradoxically, constant. The desire for continuous improvement is a realistic goal for any manager. Indeed, in an organization that can boast ISO 9000 certification, achievement of ongoing improvement will actually be a part of the retention of that certification. For the IT manager, continuous improvement can be sought through a number of means, such as:

- improved processes

- enhancing technological platforms

- increased training and a broadening of the skill-base

- personnel and HR-related initiatives (such as results-oriented bonus schemes)

These will take us so far, but their effects may be limited. In fact, against any pre-defined organization there will be a threshold beyond which process improvements cannot be delivered because the structure cannot support them. This can also be seen as true for the introduction of new technologies where it is impossible to have the necessary organization in place to provide for its utilization and support. In terms of training, skill and people-related improvements, there may very well be structural constraints which prevent individuals from maximizing their contributions based on the training they have just had, the new skills they have just acquired, or delivering against the personal incentives they have just been given. In our earlier example we referred to David's promotion from Programmer to Analyst; most likely his being trained as an analyst would have preceded this. If he had been trained but then found no analyst role available, the opportunity would have been lost. With Fred's use of the new development tools, if David had not been able to work in a 'dotted-line' fashion for another Team Leader, any advantages to be gained from Fred's broadened skill-set and responsibility would have been negated with David becoming under-employed.

Under these circumstances it is all too easy to see how we can offer opportunity on the one hand, but then prevent its successful achievement on the other. On this basis, I have to argue that in order to meet opportunities around continuous improvement, the IT structure must be flexible enough – both in terms of definition and its ability to be changed – to allow those opportunities to be taken.

3.2.2 The Need to Make a Positive Tangible Contribution

At the outset of this discourse I suggested that one of the key drivers for IT was the demonstration that it was providing value for money to the business. Given that there are increasing numbers of corporate executives who want to know exactly what they are getting for their investment in IT, this 'prove it' mentality can only grow. Symptoms of this commercial focus on the IT function can clearly be seen in areas such as downsizing, outsourcing, and an increased business control over the systems budget.

Some of the ways in which IT can increase its efficiency and demonstrate solid ROI have already been touched on, at least in passing. In the majority of instances the benchmark for proving the positive contribution will come via business cases and proposals which suggest that for an IT spend of 'X' the business will benefit to the tune of 'Y' – where 'Y' is, of course, the larger figure. This is basic stuff. The problems will always be in gaining accurate numbers for the initial business case, then attracting support for the proposition, and finally proving benefit return after delivery, implementation or whatever. The primary reason for this difficulty comes from the fact that in the majority of cases benefits are realized by the business community and not IT. If the systems function implements new ERP software exactly to time and budget, it will most likely be the business that has to deliver a large chunk of the projected benefits through a reduction in heads, working to new processes, and so forth.

There is another, more radical step that IT can take in this area which will, of course, have a knock-on effect in terms of its organizational shape. One generic business approach in terms of proving tangible benefit is, as Foote et al. (2001) suggest, to "choose your customers". An insurance company provides a range of motor cover across a wide spectrum of drivers. Despite the general trend of its competitors in at least breaking even in this area, our company is losing money. To find out why, it undertakes a systematic analysis of policy profitability based on driver profiles, primarily factors of age, sex and location. At the end of its analysis, the company discovers that policies sold to men aged 22–26 are incurring a significant loss, and all policies sold in a particular city are also demonstrating a negative return. So it decides to stop selling motor insurance to these groups; within six months its motor insurance business is demonstrating a healthy profit.

66

Table 3.1. 'Choosing Your Customers'

Current	Finance	Sales	Logistics	W'house	Total
IT resources dedicated to departmental systems	30	10	20	20	80
Cost of departmental systems	£300k	£100k	£200k	£200k	£800k
Benefits accrued from departmental systems	£450k	£300k	£400k	£250k	£1400k
Benefit–cost ratio	1.5 : 1	3 : 1	2 : 1	1.25 : 1	1.75 : 1
Number of items in systems workstack	40	60	20	40	160
Average elapsed duration to complete work item	6.7 days	30 days	5 days	10 days	16.1 avg

Future	Finance	Sales	Logistics	W'house	Total
IT resources dedicated to departmental systems	20	20	25	15	80
Cost of departmental systems	£200k	£200k	£250k	£150k	£800k
Benefits accrued from departmental systems	£300k	£600k	£500k	£187k	£1587k
Benefit–cost ratio	1.5 : 1	3 : 1	2 : 1	1.25 : 1	1.98 : 1
Number of items in systems workstack	40	60	20	40	160
Average elapsed duration to complete work item	10 days	15 days	4 days	13 days	11.9 avg

Note: A workstack item is assumed to take 5 elapsed days to complete. The average elapsed duration to complete a work item is thus the number of work items multiplied by 5, then divided by the number of resources available.

If this works in examples such as this (which is not that far removed from reality), then is there something the IT manager can take away in terms of 'choosing his customers'? Let us assume that the development arm of an IT function is aligned to business functions and sized accordingly. If we analyse how much of the company's money the IT function spends in each area and compare this with the business return, are we then in a position to 'choose our customers'?

Table 3.1 demonstrates a theoretical example and shows how, by 'choosing its customers', the IT function can improve its return to the business. By simply making an organizational change to focus resource where it can be more commercially effective – without jeopardizing critical business systems – the effect can be remarkable. Although crude, our

67

structural realignment shows an increase in benefit of over 13%, an improvement of the benefit-to-cost ratio to 1.98 : 1 (from 1.75 : 1), and an average turnaround time on work-stack items down from 16.1 days to 11.9 days.

Two points here. Obviously – and most contentiously – there is a political debate to be had within the enterprise concerned. In our example above, it will take a degree of skilful argument and persuasion to win round the heads of Finance and Warehousing – but the benefits to the business are clear enough. The IT manager would be foolish to adopt any brazen strategy without appropriate authority and support – though he might try and engineer some subtle manipulations in the background .... Secondly, for this to be successful there must be a parallel organizational shift following on from this focusing of resource or the additional benefits will be lost.

3.2.3 Recognizing the Business Drivers

In our discussion of the 'opportunity drivers' for IT, we have shown how requirements for continuous improvement and the demands to demonstrate a positive and tangible business contribution can be assisted by a reshaping of the organizational model to align with relevant initiatives. Of course the culture of the entire enterprise will have a great deal of influence here. If, for example, the company operates in a traditional and stable market where the business models have remained pretty much static for many years, then anything that smacks of radical innovation within IT may be frowned upon. Indeed, the end results may be completely the opposite to those intended.

It is likely, however, that more and more companies are adapting and moulding themselves in the light of the general business drivers they face. This will certainly be true in areas such as end-consumer retail – where the Internet has a major influence – and in start-up organizations that may wish to demonstrate outstanding speed and flexibility to accumulate market share. If the business operates in this manner and its philosophy is to seize opportunities as they arise, then there will be an expectation that the IT function can also rise to the challenge – and will be structured accordingly. In saying this, we need to recognize that opportunity-based design gives companies "the flexibility to bring the most useful resources to bear on the most promising opportunities. But the resulting organization is more complex and poses new managerial challenges" (Eisenstat et al., 2001). Note, the phrases "more complex" and posing "new managerial challenges". If this is true for the business as a whole, then what are the implications for IT?

Bringing the most useful resources to bear on systems-related opportunities could be translated as simply ensuring that existing teams of people have their priorities set appropriately. However, this does not provide very much in the way of flexibility and an ability to respond quickly to new challenges. One way of tackling this from an organizational perspective might be to have a small number of high-quality resources working with the 'opportunity focused' business teams as a kind of 'rapid response force', a unit that would proactively work with the business to seek out new systems opportunities and then bring these back into the main body of IT for delivery. Such an approach will not only demonstrate a positive response in an opportunity-driven organization, but also should assist in proving IT's contribution.

A second approach – and one that might be most suitable in a business that tailors its homogenous products to individual customers – is the creation of a front-end customer-facing unit. Business models where this approach might align well would include where product provisioning and customization via the Internet was critical, or where customers could choose from a portfolio of products and 'build' the solution that suited them best – perhaps including specially tailored billing, reporting, servicing and so forth. If you prefer, this is where the enterprise's key objective is "creating high-value solutions by integrating various products and services – even merging the supplier's and customer's operations – to solve a complete customer problem" (Foote et al., 2001). This differentiation between 'product' and 'solution' is something we will be covering in more detail later.

Whichever approach is taken – and whatever the business model or objective that acts as the driver – it is clear that, for IT to be able to provide the most effective response, there is a need to view the systems organization in the light of these demands. An assumption that a bulk-standard, traditional hierarchical model will work is naïve.

3.2.4 Allowing for Technological Change

Opportunities will arise in the technological sphere as well as the commercial, and clearly these are less likely to be driven from individual business units but rather initiated from within the IT community itself. Indeed, in an opportunity-driven modern business there may well be an expectation – potentially unstated – that the IT function will continuously innovate, proactively offering new ways of improving the efficiency of the business as a whole.

One might choose to argue that this has pretty much always been the case, and in support point to legion cases where IT has taken new concepts – such as ERP or CRM software, Internet capabilities, or new server technologies – to the business unbidden. After all, in the vast majority of these kinds of examples, where else is the driver going to come from if not the systems community itself? A Sales manager is hardly likely to appear on IT's threshold one day espousing the virtues of the new AS400 operating system he has just encountered.

Traditionally, IT has, to a certain degree, stumbled across some of their technological opportunities by accident: the licence period on their current software is about to run out, so the IT manager decides to take a look at what else the market has to offer; or the Operations manager, having responded positively to a cold-calling salesman from a hardware vendor, fortuitously discovers some new mass storage technology. These kinds of 'happy accidents' will obviously continue, but a philosophy that relies on the haphazard is hardly likely to score well when it comes to continuous improvement and innovation from the technology perspective.

It is not only the uncovering – and then implementation – of technological advances that is a cause for concern. "The problem is an inability to develop, apply and capture value from new technologies and practices, and to forge value-creating linkages between processes, business units and core functions" (Day and Wendler, 1998). This implies that simply creating a small research and development (R&D) team whose sole purpose is to proactively seek out innovation from the general systems market is not enough. Having a 'think-tank' that proposes new technological strategies and roadmaps is insufficient if these are not tied in to the 'business processes' and 'core functions' at time of inception.

To succeed here – assuming one works in the kind of company where an IT-focused R&D operation is likely to be critical – then organizationally the group that seeks out and drives these technological opportunities must be multi-skilled, comprising of not only the 'blue sky' technologists, but also those who can engage in dialogue with the business community to both translate and then gauge the value of these various advances. Again, shape is critical to success.

3.3 Business Objectives

3.3.1 How Should IT be Included in the Loop?

One fundamental issue for the systems community is visibility of business objectives – something that will apply as much in an opportunity-driven company as any other. The 'business is business, IT is IT' mentality, while being slowly eroded, does still exist to a significant extent. Keeping IT at arms length always provides the business with a convenient scapegoat for failed processes, systems and the like, whilst unfortunately preventing IT from getting close enough to try and ensure that those same processes and systems do not fail.

I have already pointed out that the big benefit winner from systems implementations will, in the main, be the business itself. This is significant for Eisenstat et al. (2001) who see that "owners of opportunities … typically exist within or alongside the business-unit structure"; and it is this structure which may be maintaining its distance from the IT function thereby preventing the "owners" of systems opportunities from actually taking ownership. Of course, whether they wish to truly own an IT initiative is another matter!

Clearly, any distance between customer and supplier is liable to introduce difficulties. If you stood outside the doors of a supermarket and shouted 'Bread!' to one of the staff inside, how fair would it be to lambast them when they brought you a sliced white loaf not realizing that you wanted an uncut granary cob? Such a scenario will not be foreign to many in IT. Business objectives may be generally known at the 'bread' level, but little further.

One would hope that the business case that actually accompanies the request for 'bread' might address the issues that exist in terms of any information gap. Very often it does not for a couple of key reasons. The first is that the business believes that 'bread' is sufficient enough instruction; after all, it is a 'systems thing' and it is the IT guys who understand systems …. The second is that the business case – often paradoxically produced by the IT function and not the business – can be so full of systems jargon (wrapped up in the language of the IT-driven initiation process) that its customers simply do not understand it. If the supermarket assistant responded with a five-minute discourse on the varieties of bread available, the flours that were used, information on nut and gluten content, weight variations, and so forth, would we not want to simple reiterate our 'Bread!' demand?

3.3.2 How Can the Organization Tie This In?

Given the scenario above, it may seem fanciful to some to suggest that modification of the IT organization structure can have any real impact on the business–IT relationship, particularly if there is a desire from either party – calculated, pathological or unconscious – to keep the two apart. Plainly, however, efforts do need to be made to improve the dialogue.

In our example above, if the store assistant had – in response to our shouted demand – actually left the store and joined us outside, and then asked us a few brief and simple questions in a language that we understood (such as 'size?', 'colour?' and 'sliced?'), then the end result would have been very different. Indeed, we would probably have been presented with exactly what we wanted. This kind of engagement is clearly some way between the 'no response' and 'five-minute discourse' options; significantly too, it also succeeds because the assistant actually leaves the store and comes to talk to us on our turf and in our terms.

I accept that the analogy is somewhat fanciful, but it does illustrate the point quite well – and from an engagement perspective suggests that the IT organization needs to have those within it who can fulfil the 'outside store' role. You might wish to argue that we already have those people in our tried and tested structures, and that it will be the programme managers, project leaders and business analysts who perform this function. But if that is the case, then why is IT still not integrated into the business? And even if these individuals are engaging (which is good) are they doing so on IT's terms (the five-minute discourse) rather than the business' (size, colour, sliced)?

This modern notion of business engagement resource is, for Eisenstat et al. (2001), an example of how we can try to ensure that (some IT) "people begin to think of themselves as entrepreneurial resources who can be applied to a range of opportunities". Not only are they opportunity-driven, they are also appropriately aligned and focused, with the kind of organizational structure and remit which allows them to step across the IT threshold. The alignment piece is undoubtedly key. If the supermarket assistant who came out to us was actually from the home-decorating department within the store, they might well ask questions about size and colour, but this might not necessarily help to ensure we got what we wanted. This person knows about paint, not bread, and unless there have been some remarkable new technological developments recently, the two are certainly not interchangeable!

3.3.3 How Does Structure Help?

Quite clearly, there are a number of ways in which modification of the IT organization can assist the relationship with the business, particularly in the engagement area, especially if properly aligned:

- Improved business understanding. By having focused engagement resource facing-off to the business community, there is a better chance of understanding the real business drivers.

- Improved business credibility. Demonstrating an understanding of business drivers will lead to a greater degree of respect being shown to the IT function. For example, why not have an IT specialist who is also a qualified accountant managing the relationship with the Finance function?

- Improved opportunity definition. With understanding and credibility improved, it is far more likely that business case production will be a joint affair; not only that, the business may well take a more active interest in the systems solutions being proposed. (In our fanciful example at the supermarket, after a few positive experiences with the 'properly aligned' assistant, is it not likely that our previous demand for 'Bread!' might in future change to 'Small granary cob, please' as we better understand – and respect – what our supplier can provide?)

- Improved commitment, both from IT into the business and from the business for the IT projects they want – and which they may be more likely to 'own'.

There will be other spin-offs too. Perhaps the engagement individual might get a standing invitation to the business function's management meeting; how better to get an insight into business drivers, and what better ambition to have? But remember, the business will not issue such an invitation to anyone who is perceived not to understand, contribute, add value, and so forth. Also, with IT being seen as more integrated, it is clear that more requests around opportunity focus and prioritization will ensue, and that – if IT is to make a positive and improving contribution – it should "not execute any service that is not specifically aligned with an identifiable business objective" (Brittain and Matlus,

2002). This latter should be a shared goal for both IT and the community it serves.

I have suggested in the previous section how by 'choosing its customers', the IT function can be seen to improve its overall 'value-add' to the business. As indicated, "changing the basis of a company's relationship with its customers may alienate some of them" (Foote et al., 2001) – substitute 'IT' for "company" and we have the picture. However, if the IT function is fully and positively engaged with all its customers, this alienation is much less likely to occur. There will always be some kind of turf war over IT resources and systems across business functions, but surely this is better fought out when based on an integrated understanding of the entire picture rather than through some kind of remote and disjointed interface (which is often held at too senior a level to really count for anything very much).

So structure is critical in this area if we are to maximize the benefits to be gained by the business from its IT investments. A little later on I will explore further potential models for engagement and alignment.

3.4 Portfolio Management

3.4.1 A Prioritization Mechanism

At the start of this chapter I set out to provide further justification as to why there was a need to consider a new way of shaping the IT function – new in the sense of a different organizational structure, as well as being constructively proactive in undertaking the task. In addition to those reasons we have already discussed, there is another which – although probably afflicting all IT departments – might not immediately appear to add any weight to my reshaping arguments. I am referring to excessive workload.

It is probably close to a universal truth that all IT functions have more work than they can handle. Against a general backdrop that may well include pressure on budgets and headcount, the list of 'things that could be done' keeps growing. Not only are these the initiatives, programmes and projects driven by the business, there will also be a myriad of 'internal' tasks that the function itself would like to see completed. Inevitably there will be too much to do. For example, how many organizations maintain work-stacks where the oldest item on the list is more than twelve months old? I once saw a three-figure programme stack where the oldest item of the two hundred requests was originally registered four years previously.

There are a number of obvious questions to be asked here. If work-stack items are so old, then surely they cannot be of any true value to the business; if they were, someone would have surely shouted loud enough to get them done. And if the stack is so long and with some truly ageing items, then this indicates that there must be something awry in the workload management process.

Some of the suggestions we have already made will obviously assist here. Getting proper engagement with the business is one key initiative. Ensuring that business cases are commercially sound before accepting them may prevent some items that will inevitably not get done from landing on the work-stack in the first place. These measures are fine and will help to ensure that in future only 'valid' items are added to IT's 'to do' list; but what about where you are right now?

Another tool that can be used is portfolio management. Essentially not an IT-specific notion, this is a mechanism or process that can assist both in the prioritization of work and, as we shall see, in make a telling contribution to organizational design. As such, it has much in common with Barton's Boston matrix approach discussed at the beginning of this chapter and earlier. Additionally, for people like Cimral et al. (2002) "Portfolio inventory analysis is … an effort to eliminate duplicate efforts", and undoubtedly there can be benefits accrued here too.

3.4.2 How Portfolio Management Can Help IT

So what is portfolio management? Based on the arguments of Cimral et al. (2002) we can regard the tool as a first-stage process that leads us from having a completely unassessed collection of items through to a position where we have far greater clarity, focus and control. It can also meet the needs of those who, like Eisenstat et al. (2001) recognize the need for some kind of visible 'initiative list' which can be used for publicity, prioritization, reporting and so forth.

As already suggested, the process as defined by Cimral et al. (2002) is not IT-focused. What follows, therefore, is my adaptation of the methodology into an IT setting. Please note that not only can we use this process to validate our work-stack items, but it can also be adopted right across the systems range to evaluate our entire resource, applications and operations infrastructure.

Step 1: Create a baseline inventory

This is essentially a fact-gathering exercise. For each individual item under scrutiny be it work-stack project, application system, or e-mail service (for the purpose of this definition, these are now called 'inventory items'), general and domain-specific information needs to be collated. It is vital to note that, if this assessment is to be a completely thorough examination of the entire IT estate, then we should include individuals who perform roles which are not directly associated with specific applications or systems, e.g. strategists who define high-level systems architectures and roadmaps. These assessments should include resource consumption estimates in terms of the headcount and budget required to keep the system operational or implement the project; for our strategist-types, this will be the cost of one full-time equivalent per role. All elements within our IT inventory must have a cost of some kind. Additionally it should be noted if the inventory item has any external influence or dependencies – i.e. are we dependant on it for selling over the Internet or linking with a supplier's own operations? – and whether or not there are future investments already committed, so not just the current cost, but committed future monies too.

We should then endeavour to make an assessment of the contribution this inventory item makes to the business. In some instances this may be available in hard terms – 'if we turn the system off we will need four more people in Finance' – in others we may struggle to get beyond stating that the item (such as e-mail) is 'strategic'. Ideally, the business should assist here; making these kind of judgements in isolation can lead to significant difficulties when trying to implement changes based on unsubstantiated findings. Finally, we should attempt to assess the visibility, profile and criticality of the inventory item from an IT perspective. For example, there will be some very low-cost, low-profile items – that small server in the corner of the computer room – which would cause havoc if they were removed.

Step 2: Conduct a portfolio evaluation

This is where, having gathered together all the prerequisite information from step 1, we make an initial assessment on each inventory item. In order to facilitate this process, it is suggested that items should be grouped logically to better enable comparisons to be made. One way of doing this is to pool the items by organizational function, i.e. all the finance items together, all logistics items together and so on. Inevitably this will leave a pool which will be 'all IT items' that have been generated by the IT function itself.

Each item now should be evaluated in terms of 'performance'. For existing systems and applications this can be based on the known; for proposed items – those in the work-stack – this will need to be based on projected performance. Resource-only roles can prove hard to assess, but the attempt must be made. Performance is judged in four categories:

a) Where the investment is 'low value', i.e. it provides a poor return for the money spent. This may best be shown as some kind of cost–benefit ratio.

b) Unhealthy investments, i.e. where the investment is failing; something that can be demonstrated by regularly missing key performance indicators (KPIs), or where estimated benefits have failed to materialize. For future projects, one might need to consider some kind of risk assessment here; how likely is it that the item will actually deliver the benefits stated?

c) Duplicate investments: quite simply where there are two or more items performing the same function, or where a new item or items would cause such duplication to exist. Note, in the latter situation we should not assume that the current item is the 'right' solution and simply reject the new one (or vice versa).

d) Strong investments, i.e. where both ROI is solid and KPIs are being met

Make no mistake, this is hard but valuable work! At the end of this step you should be surprised how few items sit in category 'd'.

Step 3: Define a portfolio plan

Now we can begin to take action based on the output from the previous step. Again inventory items should be considered in the same groupings. It is entirely likely that there will need to be significant discussion with the business community at this point; after all, in many respects we are laying down some fundamental elements of IT strategy too. The actions are based on the categories from step 2.

a) Low-value investments should be considered for either retirement (if a current offering) or elimination (by removal from the work-stack).

b) Unhealthy investment should be 'fixed'. If the assertion can be made that the investment is still fundamentally sound and can deliver positive ROI, then action plans should be drawn up to enable KPIs to be met. Execution of the action plans would subsequently move these items into either category 'a' or category 'd'.

c) Duplicate investments should be eliminated; again, keep in mind that any proposed duplicate might actually be the one to keep.

d) Strong investments should be accelerated, i.e. if the ROI from an item is positive, can it be improved further by increasing investment – money, resource – in it?

However your portfolio plan may look, remember that this is in no way a quick fix. If the methodology is being applied to a systems function in turmoil and crisis, remedial action based on the plan could take months, if not years, to execute.

Step 4: Balance the portfolio

Once you have arrived at your plan, there needs to be a step in the process that acts as a sanity check. You will need to ask yourself a number of key questions, almost certainly seeking further business input: 'If we implement the plan, do we jeopardize any critical business initiative?'; 'Do we create any single points of failure, or systems/resource gaps?'; 'Will we break any interdependencies, either current or future?'; 'Are there knock-on effects to be considered in other areas, systems, programmes, etc. if we make a particular change?'

The list will be different and to varying levels of exhaustion based on individual circumstances. At the end of this step – and through judicious amendment to the overall portfolio plan – you should have a fairly robust road map.

Step 5: Document the return on investment

How do we know if our plan has worked? There are two ways we can approach this. Firstly, as part of our portfolio plan we could define the metrics by which we will know if we have succeeded. In some cases – system retirement, for example – this will be easy enough; in others, undoubtedly less so. Taking this approach, we are likely to be getting continuous feedback in terms of improvement. If the inventory items we were assessing were all on our work-stack, then the most immediate measure will be that our work-stack should have reduced in size.

The second approach is to undertake another portfolio assessment at some defined point in the future. For entire systems installations I would suggest that six months would be the earliest – if most ambitious – deadline that could be set. Perhaps an annual assessment might suit most functions. Indeed, if timed appropriately, such an exercise could provide valuable input into the yearly departmental budgeting process.

3.4.3 The Benefits of Portfolio Management

Once we have undertaken the kind of exercise outlined above and implemented the action plans that will have fallen out, we should have helped steer the IT function in a number of ways. Indeed, in line with the kinds of opportunity-driven considerations already discussed, a well-executed portfolio management strategy will undoubtedly assist IT in terms of continuous improvement, enhancing its contribution to the business, and recognizing business change. If the latter point is not immediately evident, consider how the methodology can act as a prioritization mechanism, removing the low-value items from the IT work-stack.

It also can compliment the kind of analysis discussed earlier in this chapter (and in Chapter 1), namely the strategic value vs. operational importance Boston matrix (Figure 3.1). Some of the questions asked in step 1 of the portfolio management process should assist in defining exactly which quadrants particular elements of the IT estate actually fit into. Strong investments are, for example, likely to gravitate towards the top right-hand corner of the chart; those that are poorly performing – either in terms of KPI or ROI – will drift towards the bottom left. The movement of unhealthy investments in portfolio terms is likely to be accompanied by a significant repositioning on the matrix. Indeed, if one were so inclined, this simple depiction could be redrawn in some fashion to incorporate other elements such as the financial impact on the business; an application that scored 'low' in terms of both strategic value and operational importance but which, after the portfolio analysis, was also shown to be very expensive, might warrant very different treatment to another that scored 'low' in all three properties.

Most significantly, in much the same way as we began to argue that a simple matrix analysis might influence our organizational shape, so we can see how portfolio management can be used to drive the shape of the IT organization (The Meta Group, 2002). Indeed, the action plans that are drawn up will – on an item-by-item basis – inevitably affect the way

79

in which the function looks from a resource perspective. If a low-value or duplicate investment is to be removed (assuming this is a 'live' system) then how can this be otherwise? We are arguing for a redistribution of the resource (headcount and budget) that is currently being spent on these items; saving money is easy, in people terms this means reallocation or – the extreme, perhaps – redundancy.

Critically too, if the portfolio management technique outlined is used at the resource level – our example strategist – then we should have a dispassionate way of not only proving or disproving the value of their contribution but also, in the event that they represent a strong investment, identifying that the function needs further strengthening. Much in the same way that Barton (2002) argued that the movement of applications between matrix quadrants may point to resource flexibility, the portfolio management methodology can have a similar effect, i.e. moving valuable and expensive resource from low-value to strong investments – or to unhealthy investments in such a way as to make them strong. Barton (2002) also goes one step further when suggesting that "the portfolio technique may help resolve the age-old question of whether IT should be centralized or decentralized"; this is something I shall return to in my discussion on disaggregation.

3.5 The Customer-focused Function

3.5.1 The Front-end Trend

Throughout our discussions thus far there have been a number of themes that regularly reappear in one guise or another. One of these is the need to ensure effective and appropriate dialogue with the customers of the IT function. Indeed, we have even seen how the definition of 'customer' can, under the auspices of some e-business initiatives, be broadened to include an enterprise's end customers and suppliers. In many instances we are not talking about addressing an absence of communication, but rather an enhancement of existing dialogue. Without this, a number of IT's objectives – such as continuous improvement, recognizing business drivers, effective portfolio management – will end up being poorly executed, unsupported or failing altogether.

It is for these reasons that I would advocate the need for a new and distinct way – from a structural perspective – to ensure world-class customer engagement. This notion will, as we shall see, be more than just attempting to ensure that we point business analysts in the vague direction of customers; it is about establishing the business-focused front-end engagement process that allows IT to be integrated into the business – and which allows the business to maximize its own contribution to the successful delivery of IT systems. The 'back-end' part of the IT organization – which will, of course, still represent the lion's share of resources – will be the manufacturing and support elements at the heart of the function. However, it should be largely invisible – and irrelevant – to the business customer.

Returning for a moment to our simple bread-buying scenario from earlier, as a customer of the supermarket, I do not really care where or how the bread is made nor who makes it. I will be concerned that there is someone who can take (and understand!) my order, and that the product I receive – at the price and time agreed – meets my requirements. Apart from having a positive impression of the overall baking process, ingredients and so forth, I do not actually need to see the baker himself. It is this kind of model that can work for the IT function, but which is rarely employed successfully.

3.5.2 Problems with Traditional Silo Structures

In advocating this engagement focus, I am obviously arguing that the current model prevalent across most companies is failing. Rather than a front- and back-end split, engagement is undertaken from within a series of silos defined by application or technology – and, it must be said, defined by the IT community itself. Often the business is treated more or less as one single homogenous mass, with the customer part of the engagement process consisting of either informal IT-nominees or simply those in the business community who happen to show an interest. Figure 3.2 attempts to illustrate this.

As you can see, not only are the interfaces to varying 'depths' within the business community, one interface caters for two sets of technology ('B' and 'C'), and one application ('E') has no effective interface at all. 'Hardly likely!' you may cry; but consider e-mail as a prime example. Where is the business interface for e-mail in your own organization? And what about the help desk? Who represents the user community when defining how the help desk should work, be improved, focus its efforts, etc.?

There are intrinsically, then, a number of problems with engagement based on a silo-driven model such as this. Here are some of the most significant ones:

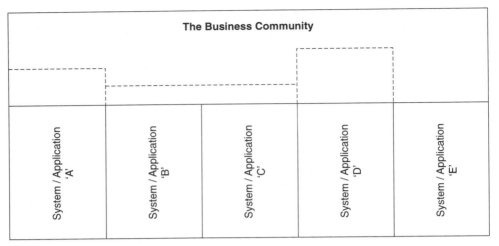

Figure 3.2. Traditional Engagement

- The wrong people from the business are engaged. More often than not key business customers who have the appropriate visibility of strategic commercial drivers and direction, and the authority to make things happen, are not formally engaged. IT will tend to nominate those individuals it knows and gets on with, rather than casting the net appropriately.

- There are varying levels of engagement. Some technology managers (Programme Managers, Project Leaders, Business Analysts) will follow a professional and rigorous approach to the engagement with their user community. For others this will undoubtedly not be the case.

- There is no mechanism for cross-silo collaboration. There will be times when a project in technology 'A' will have an impact in technology 'D'. Two levels of collaboration are required at this time: one within IT, but the second within the business community itself. A silo-driven engagement model does not provide an easy mechanism to ensure that this takes place.

- It is driven by the IT community. The inevitability here is that the model will play to the strengths and penchants of the IT function; for example, in the adoption of a project-initiation process which completely alienates the user community. As a result of this – and other failings, such as not having the right people from the business involved – the engagement process may actually serve rather to *disen-*

gage. The business will not be supportive of their IT colleagues, and there will be no bridges built.

- The model is technology- not business-focused – a spin-off from the point above, but worth making on its own as this implies that business drivers will come second to technology drivers. The business needs an enhancement to a system; the IT people know that the same system needs an upgrade to the next software version. Even though delivering against the business driver is more commercially critical, the software upgrade may get priority.

3.5.3 Broad Principles for the Engagement Organization

If we are to get the IT organization aligned in such a way as to provide appropriate and effective customer liaison, then how should we go about this? Is it as simple as making a few structural changes? Undoubtedly not. Some of the specific 'delivery' issues in terms of an engagement model will be considered in the following section; but for the moment, let us consider some of the over-arching principles that we should look to apply in our front-end function.

One way of outlining some of these key principles is to consider anti-dotes to the objections raised above against silo structures; after all, if our new model and organization is to work, then we need to have at least addressed these. The list we are working from here should not be con-sidered exhaustive. Indeed, it will undoubtedly vary from company to company. Anyone planning to instigate a new engagement model along the front- and back-end approach, should consult with their business colleagues in advance to ensure that a comprehensive list is put together containing all the failings of the present methodology from both parties' perspectives.

- Wrong people. Agree the 'level' of customer seniority and manage-ment required. Establish and agree the authority levels these people will enjoy in representing the business to the IT community. In the event of the nominees ceasing to attend meetings or beginning to del-egate to 'lower level' colleagues, the engagement process (including any steering or working groups in this area) should be suspended by the IT function and the potential lack of commitment escalated within the business.

- Varying levels of engagement. Define and agree the process by which the engagement model will operate and stick to it. This should not only include frameworks for meetings, but also processes for work-stack prioritization and things like business case templates and submission procedures. A consistent process will help everyone in IT, those 'being engaged', and tertiary parties such as Finance who may need to be involved across all channels.

- Cross-silo collaboration. Within the IT function, establish a mechanism for the various engagement parties to share information across their domains, and help the business community establish something similar on their side. (Potentially this could translate into an IT Steering Group at the enterprise level.)

- Driven by IT. A representative of the business should chair all meetings and act as the final arbitration point within each engagement area.

- Technology focused. Solved by introducing the four principles above.

One of the advantages of such an approach for the IT organization is that business engagement staff "begin to think of themselves as entrepreneurial resources who can be applied to a range of opportunities" (Eisenstat et al., 2001). Because they have stepped outside of the supermarket, they may soon learn to respond to the customer who wants bread with 'And anything else, Sir?' How else can we further this? Perhaps to get these people *really* working in the business: potentially seconded in to the business area for which they are IT's representative. If this is only undertaken for a short time, how better to get an insider's perspective?

3.6 Engagement Issues

3.6.1 Gaining Business Buy-in

In now focusing on the key engagement issues from an IT perspective, I would like to briefly consider four topics by which the success of any such model will be measured. We have already highlighted these a little earlier in one guise or another:

- Gaining business buy-in

84

- Having the necessary skills

- Demonstrating value

- Proving IT's contribution

Although the last two of these may seem very similar, in this context they are subtly different. It is also worth noting that one might choose to extend this list to include other topics – such as supplier engagement – which may be specific and critical to your organization.

In terms of business buy-in, we have indicated some of the problems potentially faced by IT's customers in the current organizational environment: being distanced; a feeling of disenfranchisement; lacking control; being without a voice, and so on. If our new engagement model is to work, then there are some specific things that we can do to address these problems.

- Give the business community (based on a logically agreed functional and/or commercial breakdown) a clear and single contact point within IT who is dedicated to their cause.

- Get the business to nominate those from within their own organization who will be the key contacts for the IT function. Suggest some kind of membership 'rotation' as an option for the business to consider – although the chairperson should change less frequently.

- Initiate steering groups or programme groups to provide ongoing direction and prioritization for specific systems and technologies, ensuring that half of the people on such groups come from business-nominated contacts, one of whom (the most senior of these) will chair these meetings. The other half will represent the systems community, and should include IT's key engagement contact.

- Ensure that the business has nominated representatives on any review or strategic initiative – such as a portfolio management exercise.

- If possible, gain agreement as to the remit, role and responsibility of any group, as well as the level of spend (resource and budget) over which the steering party has command and can allocate without any further approval. Also, within a broadly consistent framework, mutually agree the process that is to be followed to make such decisions, e.g. production and sign-off of business cases.

- On any combined business–IT working group, consider the inclusion of a resource to represent other key support functions as appropriate; primarily this is likely to be Finance and Human Resources.

- Do not meet for the sake of it! Allow the business to have a say in terms of the frequency of any formal meetings. Monthly meetings may fit the IT process model, but in times of significant challenge the business may want to meet weekly. If things are stable and quiet, quarterly may be sufficient.

From the perspective of the IT function, the responsibility of delivering all of the above should rest with the 'engagement manager' (obviously in concert with the overall IT manager where necessary). This may be very different from what currently happens in organizations from two perspectives: firstly, some of the above simply does not take place; and secondly, if it does, it will most likely be solely IT people who have responsibility and accountability for execution.

3.6.2 Having the Skills Needed

We should not delude ourselves into thinking that with the engagement manager all we have done is to define a new job role and set of responsibilities. Indeed, it is far more than that; we are looking for a different type of person – and someone that does not sit so naturally perhaps within an IT organization.

Considering the remit above, I have suggested that some of the 'business buy-in tasks' may currently be carried out by a variety of individuals in their IT roles. Let us look at the typical strengths of these people. The project manager, for example, is likely to be very task- and goal-oriented: a structured person who believes in – indeed, lives by – the plans that he puts together. If today is Wednesday, tomorrow will be Thursday no matter what anyone may say. Some of these characteristics are useful in assisting with a number of the items from our previous list; however, some may also be a liability if, in being structured and plan- or goal-oriented, there is a little business myopia and lack of flexibility. The business analyst, on the other hand, is – as you would expect – much more analytical and logical; perhaps they are likely to be driven by what is 'right', with a tendency towards the perfect solution. Again some useful attributes, but a lack of pragmatism may be a problem. The closest current IT structures may have to the engagement manager is the programme manager, responsible as they are for a range of related projects.

However, the programme manager's background is likely to be in project management, so it is possible that the same objections might apply.

So what are we looking for in our engagement manager? What are the prerequisite skills to do the job well? Here is a suggested list:

a) Personally affable, confident and approachable

b) Appreciative of business processes, drivers, and the commercial imperative (enough to be no more than one 'notch' behind the user community)

c) Not deeply technical (enough to be one 'notch' ahead of the user community)

d) Reasonably pragmatic and not technically idealistic

e) Have an appreciation of structure and process

f) Good communicator, both verbal and written

g) Capable of acting as an effective chairperson

h) Prepared to represent the interests of the business above IT (when required)

i) Personally credible

You might wish to argue that, given it is likely we will not find too many of these individuals within the IT function, that the engagement manager should be a business person. They might potentially be sourced from there, but they *must* be a member of the IT organization, otherwise you will have done nothing to provide a bridge between the two.

I would also suggest that, of the characteristics above, it is the personal rather than the technical which are the most significant for this role. Ask me to pick four critical ones, and I would suggest b, d, f, and i. To illustrate my overall point, consider this same list from the perspective of the project or programme manager; would the most important four qualities required for fulfilling this role not be somewhat different?

3.6.3 Demonstrating Value

For the more technically focused of the IT community, demonstrating the value that they bring – as individuals – is relatively straightforward. If a project is delivered on time and to budget, the project manager can claim clear demonstration that he has done his job. If program code works correctly first time and delivers exactly the functionality required by its users, then the programmer and analyst (if two separate individuals) can make similar claims as well.

These are relatively hard and fast measures of value, based on concrete deliverables. For the engagement manager (as defined above) there are going to be fewer opportunities for tangible confirmation. Partly this is due to the different nature of that which he has to deliver, and partly because the 'proof' of a valued contribution is likely to be dependant on the subjective review of his peers within the business. As Day and Wendler (1998) suggest, "only after the change has reached an advanced stage does the positive effect of the new emerging system of complements outweigh the negative effect of the disturbance to the older system that is being replaced". The engagement manager, in potentially having to see through a whole raft of issues, projects and programmes to get from the old to the new system, may well be embroiled in many months of difficulty. There may be small snippets of glory along the way, but these could well fall into the collective pot of the technicians. So how does an engagement manager demonstrate value? What is it that they deliver upon which they can be judged?

In some respects it will be what they take away as much as anything else. The engagement manager should remove pain from the business; they should take away road-blocks, ease communication, enable dialogue, and remove those business issues we referred to earlier – being distanced, a feeling of disenfranchisement, lacking control, being without a voice. If the senior business person on the other side of the dialogue can say 'I feel involved and influential; I know that the IT community now understands what I want, and that my needs are taken seriously', then the engagement person will have succeeded.

But are there some concrete things we can point to as being evidence of them adding value, or do we need to rely only on subjective opinion? Well, given that the role is a bridge between the business and IT, then the systems function is bound to be able to make some suggestions as the demonstration of value from their own parochial viewpoint, such as:

● Business processes are mutually understood by both business and IT (which for the latter will mean 'are also documented').

● Any project load or work-stack is appropriately prioritized and regularly monitored; the days of enduring shouting matches to get a job to the top of the queue are over.

- There is a clear and agreed systems roadmap based on an equally clear business vision.

Even taking just these three examples, we can spin them around and they become tangible and concrete benefits for the business too:

- The business has evidence that the IT function knows what it does and where its 'hot spots' lie.

- There is a clear project sequence based on business drivers, without any unapproved rogue 'IT projects' getting in the way.

- The business can see how systems will act as an enabler for their commercial objectives.

At the outset of any such business engagement role it will be important for all concerned to draw up a list (or parallel lists) such as these. Only then will all three parties be able to affirm that the engagement model is working.

3.6.4 Proving IT's Contribution

The demonstrating value section above is really about proving the role: the engagement manager showing how, through the various methods open to him, the link between the business and IT is made stronger, and how mutual benefit is achieved in driving system-related developments forward in an agreed and coherent fashion. We must not lose sight that the engagement manager is an IT resource, however, and that because of this there is an additional responsibility.

In many respects the engagement manager is something of a translator: interpreting business needs and challenges for the IT community, whilst simplifying systems issues in a way that the business finds they can understand. The additional aspect of the role is one of translation and communication. We said earlier that one of IT's key drivers was to prove its ongoing contribution to the business and demonstrate that it adds value. With the engagement manager in place, the IT function now has a ready-made conduit into the business, enabling the reporting back on systems performance. To this end, the engagement manager should also assume the position of 'trumpet blower' for the IT organization at a working level.

For example, let us assume that the new engagement model has been in place for a number of months and, under the auspices of one engagement person, three projects have now been completed in a single area. The business is beginning to feel reasonably confident that it now has a way 'into' the IT function, and that it is capable of getting its voice and priorities listened too. The business cases submitted for the three completed projects were, more or less, joint affairs, and the results have been – from a business perspective – satisfactory. Simplistically, the IT function has delivered what it said it would.

One might think that this would be sufficient, but I suspect not. There will be some additional details, facts, results and so forth associated with the delivery of these projects not only in terms of how the development or installation went, but in terms of the delivery of benefits too. Perhaps over the duration of the three projects the estimates provided by the IT function became more accurate, the planning a little better, the quality improved. Whatever the metrics involved, these should be used by the IT manager to assess his function.

On this basis, part of the engagement manager's remit is to 'close the loop' on completed efforts. This should take the form not only of a post-implementation review (if appropriate) but also direct feedback to the business on IT's performance. Even if this takes the relatively dry format of some simple metrics, it is IT's prime opportunity to ensure business awareness of the contribution made. Thus the engagement manager should look to provide a factual and non-subjective report back to the business at relevant times. Some examples of what this might contain are as follows:

- Estimated budget spend against actual spend. This could be for both resource and money (both for a specific project and in terms of the trend over a number of projects)

- Estimated benefits against the actual and/or re-projected benefit (this can serve as a reminder to the business that they need to keep their side of the bargain too)

- Planned dates hit, adjusted, missed

- Performance figures, for example in terms of SLAs

- Productivity figures; percentage of days spent in development, support, administration, management and so on

- Work-stack status reports; jobs by priority breakdown, average turn-around time, and so forth

The chances are that the business may not find this too exciting, but it is important that the feedback is given. In addition to closing things off, it will provide further proof (if it were needed) that the IT function was not a 'black hole' or some secret organization closed to all non-members. If these feedback reports are provided in a standard format by all engagement managers across all 'systems', then the IT manager also has ready-made input into an executive-level report of the entire function. Driven in this fashion, there should be nothing that is reported at the very top of the organization which has not been communicated to – and hopefully endorsed by – others in the business already.

3.7 Disaggregation

3.7.1 Effective Engagement and Entrepreneurialism

Our discussions on portfolio management and effective business engagement carry with them a fundamental organizational question in relation to the IT function; how much should IT be a centralized function, uniform and homogenous to all its customers, and how much decentralized? To represent the latter, I have chosen to use the term 'disaggregation', which effectively means to split a single entity into separate units. Whilst this term is more generally applied to businesses as a whole, it carries enough of the theme for me to use it here.

There are, of course, arguments for both centralization and disaggregation. There will be both pros and cons for each, and when we as individuals come to some final conclusion, the chances are that this will reside somewhere in between the two extremes of the spectrum, driven by local conditions, business culture, and so on. To illustrate this potentially insoluble dichotomy, consider our argument for portfolio management. We have suggested that this could be run across the entirety of the IT function which, by necessity, would require some form of central standards and control – particularly if the end product we are heading towards is an IT strategy. However, it is also feasible for there to be some local control too; perhaps the finance function may wish to approach their area in a slightly different way. Indeed, perhaps the finance function is the only department whose systems are currently subject to the portfolio management technique. In these two simple scenarios we could conceivably argue for both centralized and decentralized IT.

Similarly, our engagement model could be debated either way. For someone like Tom Peters (1942–) being close to the customer and learning from them leads, inevitably, towards a form of local autonomy and entrepreneurship. This can only be harnessed and maximized if, in a decentralized fashion, it is subject to hands-on, value-driven management (see Boylan, 2001). But where is the dividing line between this and the establishment of a silo mentality which, I have argued, actually detracts from effective engagement? I have also suggested that the engagement process would benefit from some form of consistency, and for many people consistency must equal central control. That effective engagement engenders a new feeling of entrepreneurship within the IT community is hopefully a positive thing; creating the organization to enable and foster this is something quite different.

Already it is evident that the centralization–disaggregation debate is a complex one. More than that, it may tend toward the philosophical rather than the tangible, and be driven more by personal prejudice and preference than anything else. Even if it is difficult, because of its fundamental importance to the shape of the IT organization, it is something we must endeavour to tackle.

3.7.2 Issues of Corporate/Central Control and Management

Much in the same way as the pendulum swings between theories of 'small is beautiful' and 'large is beautiful' at the corporate level, we can reasonably assume that the centralized vs. disaggregated models of organization will experience similar fashion swings. Indeed, in many cases decisions on the degree to which corporate or central control rules the IT roost may well mirror the enterprise-wide philosophy. If a company demonstrates tight central control, it may be less likely to allow individual functional heads to operate within structures that are radically 'looser'. Having said that, it seems reasonable to suggest that modern thinking – at least in the generic sense – is showing a preference for the decentralized argument.

It would be easy to assume that this is an entirely recent phenomenon, but that would be wrong. Alfred Sloan (1875–1966), who became President of General Motors in 1923 believed in a "policy of decentralization to individual operational areas … Each was largely independent on a day to day or month to month basis, though answerable to a small central corporate management for its performance" (see Boylan, 2001).

Although Sloan's disaggregation was at the corporate level, for many it marked a new way of considering organizational theory – something away from the strict control hierarchies that were then prevalent. Since the Second World War, this form of internal disaggregation has become the "standard model for managing very large organizations" (Boylan, 2001).

The essence of these arguments sees, for example, a multi-national conglomerate allowing each individual country unit to operate almost as an independent business, responsible for its own profit and loss performance. Apart for a limited number of corporate standards (e.g. the chart of accounts), local managing directors are free to run their business as they see fit. In part this is clearly in recognition of the potentially wide variety of unique practices and market conditions that will exist throughout the world – even, in some cases, across a single continent or even a single country. Thus, a product that sells well in North America, may struggle in Italy; a style that is adored in Southern England, may be considered completely impractical in Northumbria.

Of course, one of the greatest complaints laid at the door of the centralized model is that "too much structure and control and the organization grinds to a halt" (Eisenstat et al., 2001). The argument points to the danger of organizational paralysis – although Eisenstat goes on to recognize that "too little [structure and control] and it [the organization] is consumed by conflict". The business imperative coming to bear in recent years is the need for flexibility, speed of response, and customer focus. For example, in the United States it is now possible to customize a pair of running shoes from the likes of Nike and Adidas – a bulk manufacture off-the-shelf product that can now be made to an individual's own specification. Motor manufacturers such as Volvo are effectively offering custom-built cars – from high-volume production lines.

These propositions demand a business that is suitably nimble; an influence on IT that we have already seen. Under such circumstances, "lengthy authorization and consensus-building processes stifle initiative" (Day and Wendler, 1998) – which is exactly what is not required. If a business needs to be entrepreneurial to be successful, then it should not operate with several limbs tied behind its back. However, it is more that just the process that is an issue here; culture is important too: "Everyone knows that the corporate centre will always intervene in matters of moment. Performance is difficult to measure and individual accountability is weak, so it is impossible to employ performance-based incentives" (Day and Wendler, 1998). The suggestion is that those very attributes which are needed for success will be suppressed; not only

93

that, the corporate centre will attempt to put in place mechanisms – based on performance – that are not only destined to fail, but about which there will be a prolonged period of corporate self-delusion that they really work.

My argument here is that, if there is a need to move towards a disaggregated model at the corporate macro level in order to ensure business success, then the very same rules should be examined to see if they also apply at the micro level of the IT function. Indeed, in looking at subjects such as engagement and portfolio management, it is easy to see how an over-centralized approach could lead to the kind of "lengthy authorization and consensus-building processes" castigated by Day and Wendler, and how it will only be with a degree of local autonomy that individual 'functions' may get the most from their systems resources. To parallel the Southern England–Northumbria example, a highly rigorous, tightly controlled – but lengthy – software release procedure may be absolutely necessary for a manufacturing function, but be fatal to an Internet-driven sales force. Central IT control to this kind of level is unlikely to work in many modern systems environments.

3.7.3 The Freedom of Disaggregation/ Decentralization

If we are to support some form of disaggregated organizational model within the IT function – driven in part, as we have said, by the need to support entrepreneurial business demands – then we immediately face new and different problems. The move away from tight central control implies, by definition, that we will be introducing not only some kind of fluidity into the structure but also an element of freedom into the systems provisioning process.

From an enabling perspective, this sounds as if it could prove to be a massive step forwards. If you were a sales person who has struggled to get systems support quickly enough to positively effect customer relationships, then knowing that the IT function was going to be a) less process-bound, and b) more responsive to your requests, would seem a tremendous advance. The trick for the IT manager is, of course, knowing how far to allow the pendulum to swing away from the opposite end of the spectrum – and, fundamentally for this overall discussion, how to support this organizationally.

Freedom is all very well, but in a mission-critical technical environment it can be something of a double-edged sword. The completely wrong approach would be to indulge in a free-for-all, when effectively anything was permissible. As Pearson (1992) quite rightly says, "freedom needs to have a focus and to be well informed by strategic awareness", i.e. there will still need to be a set of rules in place that are the guiding principles and strategies by which the head of the function actually manages. For example, a system that provides a business-to-consumer (B2C) Internet selling capability may be given complete licence in terms of content, format and so forth. If the sales force or marketers choose to change the web site on a daily basis, that would be fine. What would not be so acceptable would be the use of any web site design technology they felt like, utilizing different versions of the standard corporate shopping cart software, or completely bypassing the corporate product and customer databases.

Some areas of the IT realm will be completely unsuited to any notion of free rein. This might particularly apply to enterprise-wide technologies that either lack an obvious business owner or which provide a core back-bone upon which other systems are built. e-Mail is an obvious example where 'freedom' is completely inappropriate; the security and stability of such a system will be dependent on it being centrally controlled and maintained. Similarly the IT estate may use a particular technology to provide a standard data storage platform to be utilized by all applications within the company. It would not be acceptable, therefore, for anyone to simply ignore the EMC platform and purchase a new data store for their system just because they felt like it.

In addition to getting this balance right, there are some new challenges that will need to be faced by the IT community if some form of disaggregated organization structure is put in place. Eisenstat et al. (2001) suggest two for those in the IT resource pool: the first is the need to "negotiate their own solutions to conflicts"; the second, "the new order's lack of structure". In the former case the suggestion is that where traditional hierarchical formats and associated processes would have acted as an escalation or arbitration method to resolve issues, now IT staff – and particularly those involved in the front-end business engagement piece – will themselves need to be able to resolve conflicts (both with their customers and with other areas of IS) in a positive and constructive fashion – a demand on the person rather than the process. The second challenge is essentially around the notion of freedom. To enable this new flexibility in provisioning systems, the IT structure will need to be somewhat looser; indeed, at its extreme it is possible that an organization may appear somewhat 'structureless' (though in reality it will not be). Many will find it difficult to work in such a fluid environment – which is again as much a significant people and personality issue as it is about process.

The overall message is that speed, flexibility and modern business drivers may demand a kind of freedom which, in systems terms, can only be delivered through some form of disaggregated organizational model. This is fine in principle, but it does raise new issues for the IT manager to deal with essentially around structure and process.

3.7.4 What Does This Really Mean?

This might sound theoretically acceptable, but what does it actually mean from an organizational perspective? Perhaps it is worthwhile stating what it does not mean first. It does not, for example, imply that there will be a complete absence of structure; nothing quite so anarchic could work in an environment that – to a degree – relies on a significant level of discipline and professionalism. So, from the point of view of the 'man management' aspects of the structure, there will still need to be an organogram depicting line-management responsibilities that ties the whole department together. Disaggregation also does not advocate an absence of process or procedure; indeed, in some circumstances one can envisage situations where it will in fact be more important to have – and abide by – a proven process.

So man management remains, as will the mechanisms to allow performance management, objective setting, appraisals and so forth. Process management (within the IT function) also remains, and even if it is in reduced volume it is likely to be of increased importance. Also gaining greater importance will be generic issues in both technical and non-technical spheres. The overall IT strategy will become more significant. If there is going to be a greater degree of freedom (whatever that proves to be), then there must be clearly understood boundaries within which people work. The IT strategy provides the technological boundary rope here; therefore it must exist, it must remain current, and it must be known. This latter point illustrates one of the non-technical issues that will need some focus: communication. Of all topics, internal communication is probably the one that is most berated, most needed, least understood and poorly adopted across any function in any business. If our move towards fluidity and flexibility means that there will be less top-down proactive direction (in the sense of commandment), then the general level of communication between all within the IT organization must be exceptionally good.

The kind of new organization we are proposing here is, therefore, one that focuses not on its hierarchy, but rather on the way in which its functions, responsibilities and accountabilities are carried out. For Day and Wendler (1998) disaggregation is "devolution of decision-making authority within and beyond the organization, making the controlled economy of the firm more like a market." As far as IT is concerned, the journey from the macro level to the micro leads to us supporting their conclusion that "the most important effect is to put decisions in the hands of the managers who are most familiar with the details of the business" (Day and Wendler, 1998). Thus, in the same way as we might allow the Italian branch of a corporate enterprise to make decisions affecting their local market (within a 'global' framework), so we would advocate that those involved in managing the logistics systems within a company (both IT and business) should be given a greater say in associated decision-making (within the IT strategy framework). This not only implies a 'light touch' from the IT centre, it also means that the focus for the IT organization will not be on 'jobs', but rather 'roles', 'functions', 'responsibilities' and 'accountabilities'. It is recognizing that the statement 'I am a Programme Manager' is actually meaningless; it is only when one expands the statement to say what one actually does, delivers, and is accountable and responsible for that we get any real inkling of the contribution made. In a disaggregated IT organization, we must create an environment which allows our people to do what we pay them for – to execute, deliver, own, and so forth – rather than one which restricts them because of the 'job' they have, and how this fits within a functionally sterile organizational structure.

3.7.5 Responsibility/Accountability

The terms 'responsibility' and 'accountability' are probably vastly overused, particularly in enterprises where the prevalent culture leads to the complaint by its staff that they have 'accountability without responsibility', i.e. they are charged with doing something, but not trusted enough to be given appropriate control over the tools required to actually get the job done. Normally this relates to resource and budget, although in our context the restriction on decision-making must be included. Indeed, we have already seen Eisenstat's (2001) suggested challenges – "negotiate their own solutions to conflicts" and "the new order's lack of structure" – which will, in one way or another, demand a degree of professional freedom if they are to be met.

So, if any disaggregated organizational model is to be advocated, then the ability of any resource to be both responsible and accountable for what they have been charged with is critical. Thus it is important that we are clear in terms of definitions here. Indeed, with a command structure that will provide less in the way of formal direction – 'you must do this …' – such clarity becomes doubly important.

By responsibility, I mean that an individual has a defined ownership of the delivery of an element or group of elements within the IT estate. It might be the implementation of a new billing application, the upgrade of an operating system or the rollout of new personal computers (PCs) across the organization. If any of these projects were to fail in achieving their agreed deliverables (to timescale and budget), then the failure would sit at the feet of the person who 'owns' – has the responsibility for – the delivery.

In our front-end engagement-centred functions, such responsibilities become less concrete of course. Here the engagement manager may be responsible for the relationship with his defined customer base, but it will be others who are actually responsible for the delivery of tangible systems components. Defining responsibility for a relationship will always be more challenging, but we can still include in it things that will need to happen (such as work-stack prioritization and portfolio management, perhaps) as well as the subjective deliverables based around the customers' perceptions, both of the relationship and the service they are receiving. Indeed, the latter is surprisingly easy to measure given the fashionable proliferation of satisfaction surveys and questionnaires.

For me, accountability is simply control of the pre-defined 'tools' made available for the achievement of the end goal, i.e. whatever it is for which the individual is responsible. In the case of a system implementation, the accountability would include the time of a number of resources plus an agreed pot of money to spend on software, hardware, consultancy, training, and so forth. It is here where we so often fall down. The accountability offered is nominal, not real. If a project manager, for example, sees the need to buy in an additional £20,000 of consultancy – and feels he has the budget to do so – then surely this should reside within the remit he has for the project. His responsibility is the delivery; his accountability is to remain within the budget. All too often we make people jump through hoops to get this kind of spend approved, with the ultimate decision-makers likely to be so far enough removed from the project as to render their decision an uninformed one. If we are to "put decisions in the hands of the managers who are most familiar with the details of the business" (Day and Wendler, 1998), then this is a nettle we must grasp.

It smacks, of course, of loosing control; but far from it. In the environment where the project manager does not have any real accountability for the budget, in focusing on the end deliverable he may simply keep adding things in for approval higher up, particularly if they improve his chances of success. When the project is delivered over-budget, he can simply point further up the chain and say 'well he approved all the extra spend'. On the other hand, if the project manager has the accountability for the spend and is being measured and rewarded against that criteria as well as the end delivery, then one should find that projects actually become better managed and less expensive. If he is 95% sure he will deliver on time and has to make the call on a spend of an additional £20,000 to get that last 5% – but knowing that the spend will take him over-budget – what will he do? Almost certainly not spend it. To make this kind of call, the project manager needs to know exactly what is going on, of course; and here again we may actually be increasing project control, not decreasing it.

Organizationally, allowing such freedom and responsibility has strictly no impact in terms of structure; but it does have a very real impact in the culture by which the function is run and managed, and – I would argue – this impact is incredibly positive.

3.7.6 Flexibility of Structure

Thus far, the course we are advocating for an IT organization moving forward is one which attempts to cast off formal rigidity where it needs to embrace proactive flexibility and responsiveness in order to meet the business challenges of the day. I have argued for less focus on the job titles that people possess, and greater consideration for what it is they actually do and how they do it. We have seen how traditional silo-bound structures – particularly those that have their foundations in technology rather than business – can prove a severe impediment to the delivery of what is really needed within a company. All of these things, along with other 'strategic' tools, should help IT to both prove its contribution and continually deliver value.

However, one word which keeps recurring – and which may appear as something of an anathema to any form of formal resource structure – is that of flexibility. What do we mean by flexibility in terms of an IT organization? After all, I have already said that there will need to be some kind

99

Table 3.2. Flexibility of Structure – Before

	System 'A' Finance	System 'B' Finance	System 'C' HR	System 'D' Sales	System 'E' Sales	Totals
Overall Manager	1	1	1	1	1	5
Project Manager	3	2	1	2	1	9
Technical Architect	2	1	1	1	1	6
Systems Analyst	2	2	1	1	2	8
Business Analyst	3	2	2	2	4	13
Developer	4	2	2	3	6	17
Resource available to any project	15	10	8	10	15	58

of organogram to represent a formal hierarchy of seniority and reporting; if this is so, then surely (you might want to argue) there is no room for flexibility here, otherwise we will need to redraw the organization charts every five minutes. Not surprisingly my answer is 'yes' and 'no'. 'No' in the sense that to create a structure that was in a permanent state of flux would be impractical and destabilizing. So unless we wanted to witness a slow decline in effectiveness, morale, and output, there is no room for this kind of flexibility here. Having said that, my caveat would be to assert that we should not become slaves to any organization chart; just because one is there, does not mean that it is 'right'. Indeed, when you start your next remodelling exercise you will, after all, be changing an existing structure. How often should we consider organizational change at the reporting structure level? This will be primarily driven by business demands, so there is no correct answer. Every six months or less would be dangerously frequent; every three years would be dangerously rigid.

So where is the 'yes'? Where can there be flexibility of structure? The answer is to build it within the fabric of the organization; the flexibility is overlaid there and not explicitly expressed in the structure itself. Perhaps think of resource flexibility as muscle on a skeleton (organogram); the bones are rigid, but muscle and cartilage create movement. Let us consider a simple example to demonstrate moving from a rigid silo structure to a flexible organization.

In Table 3.2 we show the 'before' situation of the applications elements of an IT function. Before the reorganization, there are five groups of resource each with a defined range of skills, capabilities and technological remit. Based on the resource within each silo, projects are constrained in terms of the numbers of people available to those teams. For example, in no one area can a project requiring more than fifteen people be contemplated unless extra resource is acquired from somewhere. After our remodelling, however, a number of things have happened (see Table 3.3).

We have refocused the teams to be aligned with business areas rather than technologies, and we have withdrawn generic skill-sets (the majority of project managers and business analysts in this example) to create pools of resource that can in effect be utilized across any technology. Based on this construction, compare the size of project that can now be undertaken across the various areas. In the Sales area, it would now be possible to run projects with up to twenty-nine people on them. This is an extreme example and would be dependant on knowledge transfer between those who were previously working on either system 'A' or system 'B'. But even if this transfer was not practical, the two resource pools still increase both capability and flexibility. For HR, the number who could support system 'C' developments has risen from eight to twenty.

More than that, by taking this approach we have been able to consolidate a little in the areas of project manager, business analysis and technical architecture. Pooling resource in this way can lead to more effective utilization – i.e. getting closer to 100% productive output (less idle time) – thereby allowing us to create an engagement manager for each area. Although this is plainly a superficial illustration and effectively considers only project managers and business analysts, it does demonstrate how it is possible to build flexibility into a structure without compromising the overall integrity of that structure from a line-management perspective.

3.7.7 Real Local Control

Does this kind of structure provide us with the local control and decision-making that has previously been advocated? To be frank, it depends – but not on the structure per se, but rather on the way it is implemented. The kind of licence needed by engagement and project managers is not about where they sit in our structure but rather the degree of authority they enjoy. Local control – which means effective, business-specific decision-making – will be influenced primarily by this.

Although this enabling culture may be the kind of environment we strive for within other forms of organization – hierarchical or flat, for example – it does not sit naturally in either. In the strictly hierarchical structure where the shape depicts not only line management but also a decision-taking tree, any attempt at local control is likely to be subverted by a strict chain of command. Additionally, this kind of structure will tend towards the silo mentality, and getting something like a project management resource pool to function adequately will be difficult. Hierarchical structures tend to revolve around control-oriented empires, which fundamentally limits the collaborative. Flat organizations, on the other hand, would appear to offer limitless local control; however I would argue that these might tend towards such a collegiate or consensus-driven unit that decision-making would actually be impaired.

To establish the kinds of control needed to meet our new vision of the IT organization, flexibility and ownership need to be happy bedfellows. One of the terms applied to structures such as this is the 'relational' organization. Whilst not denying the ultimately hierarchical nature of line management (which we can never get away from), the relational organization concentrates on how groups of people interact with each other based on what they actually do. Thus we move away from the notion that, in a single team working on a single system, an analyst works for a project manager who works for a delivery manager and so on – and towards a model which says that an analyst contributes to project 'X' which is run by project manager 'Y' for the engagement manager who owns the business relationship. Later, that same analyst may work on a different project for a different project manager and a different business stream. The relationship they possess is defined in functional terms by what they do, not what they are called or where they 'sit' on a chart.

As we have said, line management tasks will not go away. The manager of the analyst resource pool will, of course, need to pursue the same performance management tasks as if they were working in a strict hierarchical environment; however, this will need to be in concert with his colleagues managing other areas and resource pools. As Day and Wendler (1998) suggest, "capturing the value from a relational form calls for careful planning and continuous monitoring", i.e. for the management of this form of organization to be successful, there will need to be appropriate controls in place. These will need to exist not only at the performance management level, consisting of cross-team feedback and the like, but also at the overall project or programme level. If real local control is to be enabled through a structure such as this, with all associated freedoms and accountabilities attached, then management will need mechanisms in place to ensure the effectiveness of the decision-making process.

3.8 Alignment Models

3.8.1 Front-end Alignment

The move towards a relational IT organization no longer lining up behind specific technologies – particularly in terms of business applications – requires that we address the issue of alignment. In our new structure, exactly how should the sub-groups within the IT department be focused? We have used some crude examples thus far in attempting to illustrate how we might make a transition away from the silo mentality, and now we need to consider this in more detail.

Those who have identified this imperative have, like Joseph Pine, recognized that customers are now seeking a specialized, customized, and tailored service. This means that an IT organization must be able to a) recognize, b) interpret, and c) respond to such demands. These kinds of notions, which also suggest an increasing importance in 'how' something is carried out, is fundamental to those who subscribe to the notion of the "experience economy" (see Boylan, 2001). Our suggestion as to the creation of new roles such as the engagement manager fits well within this model, particularly as success of the individuals concerned will, in part at least, be governed by the kinds of 'experience' they provide to their immediate customers.

So how might we wish to align our front-end IT functions? There are three options I am going to briefly discuss here:

- To the business unit – i.e. to mirror the internal structure of the organization
- To the end customer – i.e. to reflect customers and customer groupings
- To products – i.e. to support specific products or product groupings

In order to facilitate this analysis, I have chosen to concentrate on a subset of a fictitious enterprise. The individual elements contained within this subset are as follows:

Table 3.3. Flexibility of Structure – After

	Finance Systems	HR Systems	Sales Systems	Project Manager Pool	Business Analyst Pool	Totals
Overall Manager	1	1	1	1	1	5
Engagement Manager	1	1	1	0	0	3
Project Manager	1	1	1	5	0	8
Technical Architect	2	1	2	0	0	5
Systems Analyst	4	1	3	0	0	8
Business Analyst	2	1	2	0	7	12
Developer	6	2	9	0	0	17
Resource available to any project	29	20	31	6	8	58

Note: the total resource available to any one project includes all those within the business alignment area, plus all Project Managers and all Business Analysts (excluding their managers) from their respective pools (i.e. an additional 12 resources).

- Within the organization itself, in addition to the IT function there are the following business units: Sales, Product Management, Finance, Human Resources and Logistics.

- At the customer level, there are three logical customer 'groups' plus one very large individual customer.

- At the product level, I am working on the basis that there are four key product groupings.

The next three sections will demonstrate a) how the IT function can be aligned with each of these in turn, b) the circumstances under which you might want to do so, and c) the impact such an alignment might have, particularly on the remaining elements within the overall business flow.

3.8.2 Alignment by Business Unit

Setting up their function to focus on internal partner business units is perhaps the most common alignment model adopted by IT managers today. In this example we would see the engagement function split into five units, with a manager owning the relationship with each of the internal customer units. The shape of the IT function sitting behind the

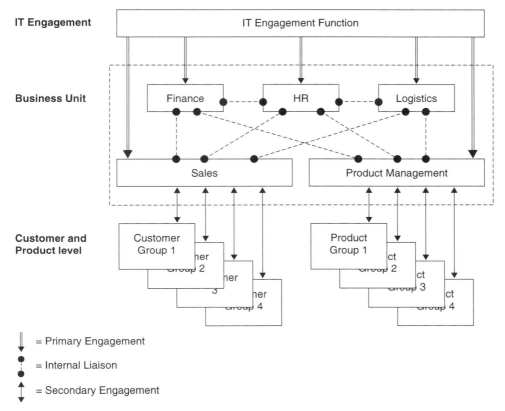

IT Engagement

Business Unit

**Customer and
Product level**

= Primary Engagement

= Internal Liaison

= Secondary Engagement

Figure 3.3. *Business Unit Alignment*

engagement managers can, of course, vary, but it may well look something like that outlined in Table 3.3, i.e. groups of dedicated resource focusing on related systems with supporting pools containing generic skill-sets.

As we can see in Figure 3.3, around the business units themselves there will obviously exist a number of internal interfaces at the process level; these will undoubtedly cascade into the systems arena too. This implies that there needs to be some co-ordination between the engagement areas and the individual business units themselves in order to ensure that all systems developments fit not only within an overall IT strategy, but also together as a cohesive business whole. Again, this is something we have already suggested.

Alignments such as these would, in addition to being the default (i.e. the 'easiest' to implement), be most appropriate under two circumstances. Firstly, where there is a wide diversity of customers who do not easily fit into groupings and where none of these are excessively large or influential. Perhaps one good example is a business that sells to individual end consumers, i.e. the general public. Here systems would be most likely to maximize their 'value-add' by being focused on internal processes and procedures to maximize corporate speed and efficiency. The second – and possibly parallel – requirement is that there are no distinct product groupings either. By this I mean that the products sold to end customers cannot be put logically together in such a way as for each product portfolio to be different from the next. An Internet-based bookseller might be a good example here. Not only are the customers a large amorphous mass, the products – although divisible into categories such as 'food', 'novels', 'health' and so on – are all subject to the same business processes, i.e. there is nothing unique about them. Setting up our engagement model in this way means any influence that needs to be brought to bear from either the customer or product side will be driven through the sales and product management functions respectively.

3.8.3 Alignment by Customer/Customer Group

Our second example, that of aligning the IT function with our end customers, is probably a less common approach. Here, IT engages with specific and logical customer groupings and, in instances where there are large enough individual customers, directly with those single corporate entities. Under such circumstances we are obviously not talking about an enterprise that is in a business-to-consumer market.

Perhaps the most obvious example of such an alignment would be where the business is focused on selling to vertical industry sectors. Thus our groupings may be Financial Services, Government and Telecommunications, whilst our single large customer could be one of the giant multi-national corporations who spend millions with us on an annual basis. This kind of model recognizes that, whatever our product, there are discrete requirements from our three logical groupings which will require differing support from both a front-end and back-end systems provisioning perspective; potentially, billing might be an example of where requirements on IT systems might diverge by sector. Additionally, the model recognizes that our global conglomerate is so important to the enterprise as a whole that the business would do almost anything to keep this customer happy.

Given this scenario, the primary business drivers would come from these customer sets. For the IT function, the main engagement would be through the sales function supporting the groupings shown; direct liaison with end-customers may be necessary in the event of collaborative e-business systems or extranet-type initiatives, but this would probably not be the norm. Given that our company may well be sales-led, engagement with other business units – Finance, HR, and so on – is likely to be slightly subordinate to our sales focus; that is to say, the IT function may well add most value to the enterprise through its customer-driven engagement. This model is shown in Figure 3.4.

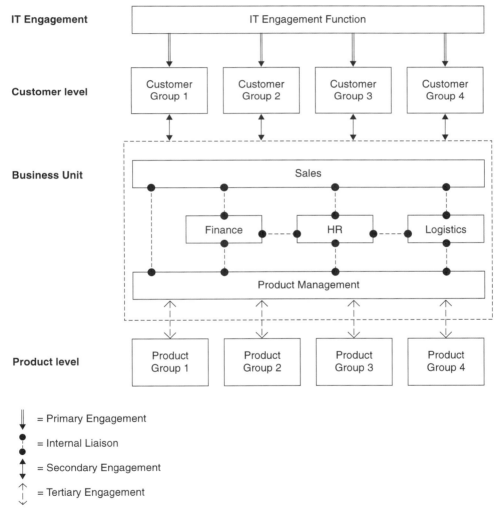

Figure 3.4. *Customer/Customer Group Alignment*

As you can see, in this example our product portfolio is relegated to the least important engagement element for the IT function. What kind of organization might fulfil this profile? Perhaps a training company who offer specialized and tailored customer services and management training to other businesses, including the supply of on-line training and assessment materials which could be tailored to the meet the needs of a customer or customer grouping. In this case, the sector-by-sector approach is valid, as requirements will clearly vary between them. The product set will not be an IT-dependent base product as most of the IT work would be in customization at the sales end. Additionally, the kind of IT support provided to the trainers themselves could effectively be quite limited.

3.8.4 *Alignment by Product*

Our final study here is based around an operation where the most critical element in the entire business proposition is the product set. An obvious example of a company in this environment would be a software development company whose offerings to the market were based around four core products. Here, the IT support for these products – particularly as 'manufacturer' – would be absolutely critical to business success. On this basis, it makes sense for the IT manager to align his function to those critical product groupings.

In this instance, the key relationship will be through the product management function that will be handling the ongoing development of each software product throughout its life span. As with our previous example, the importance of this specific engagement overshadows that between IT with other business units. Again the reason is clear; it is in the critical area of the software products that IT has most value to add.

Figure 3.5 demonstrates this model. It is not surprising that it looks remarkably similar to that shown in Figure 3.4, the difference being the reversal of roles for customer/sales and products. In our product-centric world, the job of the sales force is to sell the 'vanilla' software products as developed and maintained within the product portfolio. In this example enterprise, customers would take the software 'out of the box', buying licences and support as appropriate. Indeed, companies with a portfolio of desktop applications products – grouped into Operating Systems, Word Processing tools, Database tools and Communications tools – might well fit this shape of engagement. Of course, it is highly unlikely that in any 'real' business we would be able to delineate these models in quite such an exact fashion. One would need to overlay a number of realities – the 'first among equals' status that may exist in peer business units – as well as other elements of the IT estate, such as Operations, help desk and so on.

Indeed, if there were a need for a 'rule of thumb' in terms of where the primary engagement focus for an IT organization should be, one should look initially to that aspect of the business which is most critical for

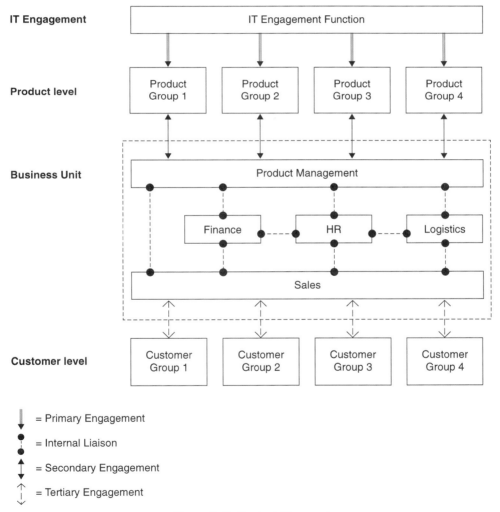

Figure 3.5. *Product Alignment*

continued commercial success. For our training organization, it is end-customer focus; for the software company, the product is king. Given that this will decide where the real business drivers will emerge, it also may well suggest the areas where the IT function can make the greatest contribution. In other companies, where both product and customer are vital – but neither dominant – then an alignment based around the internal business units might well prove to be the most appropriate model; after all, this still allows for both product and customer to be represented by the sales and product management functions.

Solutions vs. Products

4

4.1 Introduction

4.1.1 The Solutions vs. Products Issue for IT

One of the increasing trends faced by businesses in the new Internet-aware, 'always on', experience economy, is the move away from supply of what might be regarded as 'products' towards the provision of 'solutions'. As we suggested in our previous chapter, customers are now seeking a specialized, customized and tailored service – hallmarks of solutions rather than products. Simply offering customers something off the shelf is, in many industries, no longer sufficient. Indeed, one could consider markets that are fundamentally product-driven and yet find examples of 'solutions' creeping in – even in the business-to-consumer sector.

Internet-based retail and service organizations now offer their customers the ability to customize and personalize their interface; loyalty cards from stores mean that people are effectively purchasing more than just a single item when they choose any individual purchase; combination offers in retailers – and those targeted at specific customers via data collected on them – all seek to 'bundle' products into something more. In other industries – the software and consultancy market being an obvious case in point – purchasers are seeking more than just the 'vanilla' product. They want customization, consultancy, support, systems integration assistance and so on. In fact, it could be argued that one of the key attractions of any outsourcing deal is the potential to purchase a solution rather than just a product or service.

This obviously puts some pressure on a product-driven business, and, considering our recent arguments on the engagement process, pushes the alignment model towards the 'customer is king' proposition. For the IT service, similar pressure is inevitable, if not visible already. Many elements of the IT estate are traditionally provided as a 'product' – even those that may, as in the case of the implementation of a new system, appear to be otherwise. If the end deliverable is a new set of application programmes and nothing else, it is a product. The e-mail system can be seen as a product. Provision of Internet access, a product. However, with IT's customers being exposed to more and more 'solutions' offerings in their daily lives – and with the pressure from new business challenges for flexibility, speed, tailoring and so forth – the demand on the function for solutions and not products can only grow.

For Foote et al. (2001), the need is to "build value propositions for customer outcomes" – which is much more than simply offering a selection of products and walking away. If the product to be provided by the IT function is a new ERP system, for example, where is the value proposition if this delivery is not accompanied by new working practices, processes, full training, additional interfaces to other systems, or simplification of the systems landscape? When we go into a sandwich shop for lunch, we order a 'solution'; we do not expect to be given two slices of bread, some butter, cheese, salad, and a knife, and then told to 'make it ourselves'. More and more, therefore, business drivers are pushing IT away from their traditional products and this, in turn, must also include any traditional IT organization that is not shaped to deliver solutions.

Foote's (2001) argument, that "to succeed with solutions … [one] must question product-focused business practices" indicates how far the new IT organization must go if it is keep up with the customers it serves. And let us not forget that these customers can be internal, end-customers, and other partners too. For some businesses the requirement will be to create "high-value solutions by integrating various products and services – even merging the supplier's and customer's operations – to solve a complete customer problem" (Foote et al., 2001). Traditional product-bound IT organizations will surely struggle in this space.

4.1.2 Traditional Organization Focus

My suggestion is that 'traditional' IT organizations are based around the provision of a suite of products to the customer (where a 'product' is in this sense an element within the IT estate). As an illustration, let us assume that we are dealing with a relatively traditional business whose IT function is there primarily to serve internal business units, i.e. the function does not provide a critical service delivery function in either the product or end-customer areas. As such, the structure of the department follows a standard breakdown; namely, a split between applications development and operations. In the former, individual teams are

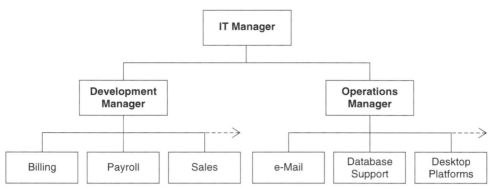

Figure 4.1. A Product-focused Organization

dedicated to the various core systems in use across the business; in the latter, the breakdown is fundamentally defined by technology and platform. (Figure 4.1 gives a simplified breakdown of this structure.)

As we can see from this shape, the focus for each of the various teams is pretty well defined, and this targeting is based around the delivery of a product: the billing engine, the payroll system, the e-mail platform, various database services. The work-stacks that exist for each of these entities will be concerned with modifications or enhancements to the products that the teams support; perhaps a new report from the payroll system, or an upgrade to the e-mail platform. These individual elements are not solutions – and, in the vast majority of cases perhaps, we should recognize that the business served by the IT function does not actually ask for solutions. More often than not, the process of analysis that is undergone with business and IT working in partnership will deconstruct any required solution into technical product components for delivery, i.e. the need to provide an order-to-cash process-based solution with appropriate systems support will be translated into a series of individual application (sic 'product') modifications. This happens because a) IT professionals are driving the analytical work, and b) they fail to understand either solutions provision or the way the solution has been articulated to them.

The suggestion made by Foote et al. (2001) – that "even when product-focused companies do summon the courage to develop a solutions strategy, the organizations often fail them" – is interesting on two counts. Firstly because there is the recognition that the structure of the IT function will be product-based; and secondly, in implying that an IT

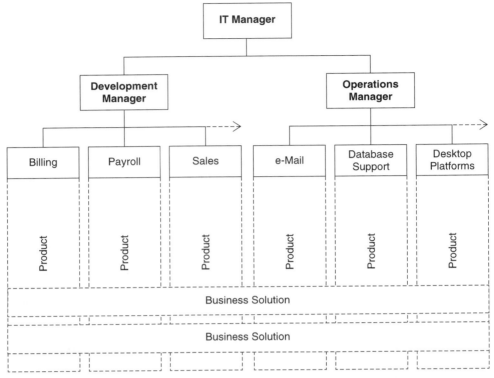

Figure 4.2. *Solutions vs. Products Organizational Shape*

strategy is not a "solutions strategy" but rather one based around the implementation of a technical (product) roadmap. Even when "managers start not with a product but with a desired outcome for a customer" (Foote et al., 2001) their existing organizational models – being product focused – create a disjoin that can only result in the successful implementation of a business solution if given a considerable slice of luck. If the IT manager is to be successful as a 'solutions provider', then they must have the organization in place to support such deliveries.

4.1.3 Front- vs. Back-end

Part of the issue here is the silo tendency that traditional organizational structures can incubate, as we have already seen. One way of looking at this in the light of what we have said above is to regard product delivery as a 'vertical' function for the IT department, whereas the provision of solutions sits on the 'horizontal' across the organization (see Figure 4.2).

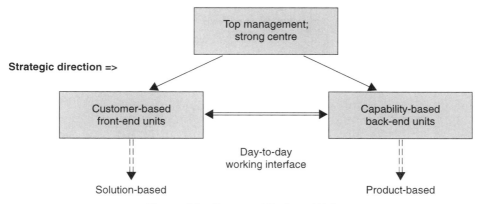

Figure 4.3. *Front- and Back-end Units*

In representing the difference between product and solution delivery in this way, we can readily understand the disjoin between requirement and delivery capability, should one exist. The solution – which in all probability will involve a business process sitting across multiple areas of responsibility within IT – can *only* be deconstructed into component technical parts for the product silos to take on. Without a supportive organizational shape, where should the owner reside if we were to deliver one of the solutions in Figure 4.2? Not only does this product–solution challenge demonstrate issues with such a 'normal' structure, it also highlights the demand for engagement and ownership at the right level and within an effective and enabling structure.

One way to address this dichotomy is to reform the organization in recognition of the solution–product split; after all, not everything demanded from the IT function will be a solution, in the same way that 100% delivery of product will be inappropriate. This could be achieved perhaps with "strong 'front-end' units responsible for developing and delivering integrated solutions" (Foote et al., 2001), whilst still recognizing the important place product ('capability') delivery has within the IT function. This model is shown in Figure 4.3.

Here we can see the logical breakdown – from an organizational perspective – of a mechanism that allows the IT manager to realize the solutions delivery challenge. Based on what we have said thus far, it is clear that the engagement function would sit within the customer-based front-end units and, conversely, those strictly product-based operational elements of the estate – such as database management, perhaps – would reside in the capability-based back-end units. How the remainder

115

of the function is 'divided up' between these two core blocks is open to some debate, particularly as taking the easy route and calling them 'applications' and 'operations' may simply move us back towards the very silo-based model from which we are trying to remove ourselves.

Undoubtedly there is no easy answer here, and even though taking the applications–operations approach may serve as a starting point, it should be challenged hard. Take e-mail as an example. In our earlier diagram this was shown in the operations (product) area. But what if integrating e-mail functionality into our Internet B2C applications was critical to providing business solutions aimed at our end customers? Or perhaps we might wish to regard the HR-related systems as product not solution; after all, they are unlikely to form part of any business-critical process, and if their remit is solely staff records and payroll, then might they not be seen more as product delivery? Although the mix is likely to vary between IT departments based on the businesses they are supporting, this model does illustrate that there will need to be definite processes to glue together the two parts of the IT delivery function. However the organization is finally defined, dialogue between solutions and product elements will be inevitable, and the mechanism that enables this will be key.

Finally here, although we are suggesting this kind of breakdown in order to better provide for solutions provision moving forwards, there is an argument – again made by Foote et al. (2001) – that "the purpose of the front–back split is as much to strengthen the product side as to create a new focal point for solutions". This is undoubtedly true. For any function within the IT organization, knowing where it sits in relation to its peers has to improve clarity; and with the right processes and procedures sitting between the various elements, managers of those individual areas will certainly have a better understanding as to what is expected of them.

4.1.4 Relationship with Disaggregation and Alignment

This kind of front-end/back-end approach also echoes the alignment discussion from our previous chapter where we talked about options for the engagement function in being aligned with internal business units, customer-focused or product-focused. Being able to make that decision will undoubtedly help to know which side of the solution–product divide various parts of the IT organization should sit. But consideration of solutions' delivery is undoubtedly more than that; it is also influenced by the kinds of customer-driven demands – the need for flexibility, speed and responsiveness – that we have continually echoed. Product provisioning is relatively mechanistic; the delivery of solutions much less so.

In consideration of the opportunity-focused organization, the research undertaken by Eisenstat et al. (2001) recognized that "to create account-ability around opportunities, most of the companies we studied have established permanent opportunity-based units ... or solutions teams". Thus, in order to be entrepreneurial, there was an explicit undertaking in some businesses to proactively harness the opportunity culture through an organizational change that supported the prerequisite engagement, alignment and solutions-based structure. If this approach is valid at the macro level, then, as I have already suggested, the same philosophy can apply within the micro-level IT function.

In some cases such an approach can have a significant impact within the IT department itself, depending on what functions/roles the front-end engagement units adopt and how far along the disaggregation spectrum one chooses to place them. Taken to the extreme, customer-focused front-end units "have no product responsibilities or even loyalties" (Foote et al., 2001); the argument here being that, if the remit of these groups is to provide the right solution irrespective of almost any constraint, then why should the provisioning agency be mandated as only being the other elements of the same internal IT function? In an outsourcing scenario such an argument is perfectly invalid – indeed, its opposite is almost a prerequisite: where a business is pursuing a ruthless outsourcing model for IT service provision, its IT function may consist only of engagement units. For a function where there is either a balanced provisioning approach or the local IT department is the sole supplier, there will undoubtedly be an impact if the disaggregation approach does not match the overall remit of the department. If customers are allowed to go elsewhere, then such freedom will almost certainly undermine any defined IT strategy as they ride roughshod over any internal procedures defined to ensure the overall integrity of the IT estate.

Undoubtedly there is a balance to be struck here; a balance that attempts to ensure the right degree of freedom and flexibility, the correct engagement model, quality support for both solutions and product provision, and a suitable approach to disaggregation. My argument is that shaping the IT organization in the most appropriate fashion can act as an enabler for all of these elements. Not recognizing that these four atomic-level elements need to be brought together in harmony will lead to an inevitable conflict of interest that could almost be as counter-productive as not recognizing that they exist in the first place. To a certain degree, the new IT structure, once it is in place, could act as something of a catalyst for a virtuous circle. For example, "product units must become more flexible and open so that they can respond to the front-end units' incessant demands for resources" (Foote et al., 2001), i.e. where solutions' provision both drives and depends on elements of product delivery, the ability for the capability functions to raise their game to meet the new challenges they are being set will only enhance the overall delivery and efficiency capability of the entire function.

4.2 IT Services

4.2.1 Articulating What IT 'Does'

Without question one of the problems facing any IT function is getting its business customers to understand what it does and how it does it. Perhaps such a generalization applies less in the product-driven environment of, say, the software house, but it is certainly a valid observation in the majority of cases. If IT is not 'understood' it will be for two reasons: firstly, the function either fails to, or finds it difficult to, articulate its purpose; and secondly, because its customers are not engaged and do not actually care. In a situation where we are remodelling the organization and inventing new customer-engagement functions or processes to improve speed, flexibility and response, it is important that the business understands where we are going. After all, a new engagement function of which only IT is aware will be as effective as a one-armed handshake.

If there are discretionary 'transform the business' investments/solutions aimed at growth and/or new ventures whose success demands the IT organization be more flexible, open to influence and better able to respond, then any changes in IT shape specifically undertaken to meet these demands must be communicated (The Meta Group, 2002).

The articulation of what IT actually does and outlining the services it provides is always important; obviously it is even more so where a tighter relationship with its customers is critical to their mutual success. What can IT do, then, to foster this greater understanding? Simply publishing the new organization chart to some corporate intranet will certainly not be enough. As we have said, our new functional shape is more about what people do and they way they do it rather than their job title. The organogram will show reporting lines of course, but how can it articulate the difference between solution- and capability-provision? Make no mistake, having no one outside IT who understands what it is about can only lead to failure. If you are playing football and have been given a specific position and remit on the playing field, how successful are you likely to be if your team-mates are not aware of what your role is supposed to be?

So we are looking at marketing the IT function and some internal PR (public relations) – to be frank, even selling it, too. Who is best placed to undertake these kinds of tasks? Well, obviously the IT manager will have needed to sell his organizational ideas to his own manager in the first place; in all probability it will then be up to these to take the message to the senior echelons of management within the business. They will need to explain not only the structure and why it is shaped the way it is, but also the strategy that lies behind it. They will need to emphasize that the new shape is specifically aimed at providing an improved service to its customers, and – perhaps most significantly – they will need to explain what is needed from the business in order for this to be a success. Implementing an engagement methodology where business partners simply fail to turn up for meetings and just do not buy in to the process is worse than having no such methodology at all.

At the working level, once the message above has been delivered, the engagement managers will need to initiate the relationship with those nominated from the business to complete the handshake. It would be a mistake (all too commonly made, I suspect) for IT's engagement manager to expect things to work from Day One simply because he understands his new remit and the procedures he needs to follow. It will take some little time for non-IT peers to get a grasp of the part they have to play in this brave new world – particularly as the briefing they receive from their managers may be perfunctory. So the message is that you cannot assume that the job is done when the new organization is drawn-up; without the subsequent PR and sales activity, it is likely to have only minimal positive impact.

4.2.2 'Solution' focused; Perception-driven

One of the hardest things for the IT community to articulate will be the shift towards delivering solutions. For those that have tried to provide a view on the services offered by IT in the past, this may prove doubly difficult. After all, it is likely that any 'service catalogue' produced will have failed to achieve its laudable goals because a) it became quickly out-of-date, b) it was used only by the IT function itself, or c) it was effectively meaningless to the business. Why, in this last case, might this have been so?

If we return to our simple notion that IT products are vertical and solutions are horizontal, the service catalogue as many now understand it would have been based around the vertical capability. Any attempt at putting a 'business spin' on the definition is likely to have either been limited by IT's interpretation of what the 'system' did for the business or hampered by the articulation of a service level agreement (SLA) which may have never been monitored or reported on. For a service catalogue to be of value to those who use the services provided – be that solution or capability – then it will need to be written and presented in such a way as to be of use to its user community. Thus, it is of more value to someone within the HR function to know that the payroll system can provide sixty-eight standard reports and has a 'what if' mechanism to enable bonus payment calculations, rather than the fact that it runs on two Pentium-driven servers running version 6.2.1a of a particular operating system. A positive spin-off here is that the general functionality of the system will change less frequently than the technical environment (that upgrade to 6.2.1b …) and therefore make the catalogue easier to maintain.

Articulation of what being 'solutions focused' actually means will, in all probability, need to come more from interaction at a personal level. It may be possible for the service catalogue to articulate what happens on the vertical, but systems support for the 'prospect-to-order' business cycle will surely begin to veer into the realm of business process. This will be fine given two caveats: firstly, that these processes can be related to systems delivery (i.e. they do not sit outside the IT realm as some form of idealistic business approach that bears no resemblance to what actually happens); and secondly, that the IT function is organized in such a way as to support this cross-vertical view. This is something I will address in a moment.

Finally here, having outlined some of the issues for the IT function in articulating the services it endeavours to provide, we need to recognize that the dialogue will need to be two-way, i.e. we should ensure that there is customer feedback in terms of how the department is performing. Make no mistake here, no matter how clear we may be in explicitly defining services from both a solution (horizontal) and capability (vertical) perspective, how the function 'scores' with the business will be largely driven by perception. This does not make the feedback invalid; neither does it suggest that the input will be of no constructive value. What it does mean is that the IT manager will need to define and agree a mechanism which allows his customers to provide their comments on his services in a way that is acceptable to them and meaningful to himself.

There can be no right answer here – except in that it must be done! My primary concern is simply to ensure recognition of the fact that, no matter how specific the IT community may want to be in terms of stating factually the function, content and quality of its services, its customers' feedback is likely to be based on their own criteria, process and perception. A simple example: One IT manager's offerings is e-mail. During a three-month period he is able to report 99.8% availability – a performance that sits well within his SLA. At the end of the period he coincidentally surveys some of his customers as part of a regular feedback process and is told that the e-mail service is 'awful'. How can we square this with 99.8%? Easily – if the 0.2% downtime actually occurred as a single significant loss of service at a critical time during an end-of-month working day. Of the two views, the 'awful' tag is the one that will carry most weight.

4.2.3 Organizational Impact

Additionally we might choose to provide a narrower definition of 'IT Services'. Thus far I have considered it as the depiction of the breadth of that which the systems function brings to the business. However, restricting this to a more specific meaning of 'services' perhaps allows us to create a systems triumvirate: Services, Delivery Management, and Operational Management. There is some merit in such a breakdown as it allows us recognize the discrete drivers for each, as well as identifying how our organization will be impacted in turn.

Table 4.1 attempts to show how, for each of these three major areas of the IT function, the organizational drivers, focus points and key measures will differ. We have already begun to suggest that the services element is about business engagement with a focus on solutions provisioning, and that success will be relatively subjective. Operationally it is easy to see how a stable organization focused on product and service will be essential; and in the development or manufacturing area, how there will be a

Table 4.1. IT's Organizational Drivers

	Organizational drivers	Key focus	Key measures
IT services	Customer alignment	Solutions	Perception
Delivery Management	Flexibility & speed	Solution & product	Results
Operational Management	Stability	Product & capability	Service

need to grasp both solution and product, with tangible delivery being the most critical result.

I will return to both of these latter two areas in a short while, but for the moment what would reside within a 'services' remit? Business engagement is the obvious first candidate we have already covered. A little earlier in this section I also made reference to business process analysis, and how, if the IT function is going to be able to support the delivery of cross-vertical solutions, it would need to consider having people who could work within the horizontal layer and whose skills would most likely be technology independent. So how might our services group look?

- Business engagement – Providing the strategic link or bridge between customer functions and IT, acting as the key communication point.

- Programme management – A number of people who represent the business within the day-to-day management and delivery of a suite of related IT projects. This might be particularly relevant where delivery of a business solution represented – to the IT community as a whole – a series of product-related projects. (It is possible for a single individual to occupy both engagement and programme roles.)

- Business analysis – Those who can work with the user community to assist in both translating current processes into systems requirements, and who can also help the business to define and implement new procedures with a view to getting the most from systems implementations.

- Training – A small group capable of delivering IT training to the end user community, not only on desktop tools, but also in support of major programme and project implementations.

In delivering these kinds of functions, we can see how, by defining their shape, we are putting together the concrete foundations for the final organization. Thus, we can ask specific questions such as: Do we have engagement and programme management as dual roles undertaken by single individuals, and if so, how will they be aligned? Do we need a pool of business analysts, or is there an argument to have these work in tandem with the engagement managers, or even allied to the development teams?

4.3 Delivery Management

4.3.1 The Manufacturing Element; A Stability/Fluidity Mix

The second element of our triumvirate to consider is that which translates the needs and requirements of the business into tangible systems deliveries. Earlier, I referred to this segment of the IT function as 'manufacturing' and in many respects this parallel is not a bad one, particularly if we regard the generic process as one of taking a raw material of some kind and then effecting change in order to produce something else. IT developers work within this kind of schema with their raw materials being technical tools – hardware or software – and their own knowledge and talent – the output being a technological component which assists and supports a business process.

The manufacturing metaphor is useful in other senses too, bringing with it notions of things like testing, inspection and quality control – all of which can have an impact in the IT development area. At the generic product level, W. Edwards Deming (1900–1994) argued that businesses should "cease dependence on mass inspection; build quality into the product in the first place" (see Boylan, 2001). Not only the historical objective of 'zero defects' in IT systems, but also the present need for fast and 'right first time' application deliveries lends support to Deming's arguments, with "product" extending to "process" too. However, if we are to "build quality in", then we have to face up to the organizational implication of doing so. An outsourcing strategy allied to the same mantra is echoed in a plea to "end lowest-tender contracts; instead, require meaningful measures of quality along with price" (Boylan, 2001). If we are to comply with this notion, there will be some impact in the shape and skills needed within the IT function.

Of course, establishing any degree of quality or certainty within the manufacturing process effectively implies the need for a degree of consistency or stability. If, for example, the way a code generation tool was used changed regularly or the rules for unit testing application components were in a constant state of flux, then it would be difficult to establish the kind of benchmark processes needed to drive any kind of quality assurance programme. On this basis, the need for stability is clear. However, we have already argued that, in order to meet business demands for fleet-footedness in the delivery of business applications, the IT delivery function must be flexible enough to be able to respond accordingly. In our examples in the previous chapter (Tables 3.2 and 3.3) we saw how building flexibility in to the fabric of the delivery organization could improve responsiveness. In the development areas of the IT function therefore, we might reasonably argue for a mix of both stability and fluidity; and this is something that our organizational structure will need to embrace.

4.3.2 Both Product and Solution; Results-driven

Making such a statement may seem like simply arguing for the best of both worlds – as well, perhaps, as setting out organizational goals that cannot be met. However, some of the suggestions already made – for example around the pooling of generic resource skill-sets – demonstrate that there is much that can be done to address potentially conflicting demands. Of course in the delivery area another pair of critical drivers suggest a similar issue; these represent the need to be both solution- and product-focused.

Let us assume that IT is charged with delivery of appropriate systems technology to support a solution that spans a number of business areas. In addition to some horizontal process-related changes, this solution can only be delivered via the introduction of new individual application modules that reside across a number of discrete systems. In order to ensure that the solution is successfully delivered as a whole, the manufacturing element of the IT department will need to be able to operate both horizontally and vertically, i.e. at solution and product level. How might this be achieved?

The vertical contribution will be relatively straightforward. If the systems concerned are, say, the sales system, the finance application, and the product management suite, then it is likely that there will be individual teams of people with specific technical expertise centred on those systems. Excluding the programme or solution management element (which will be managed from within the services or engagement

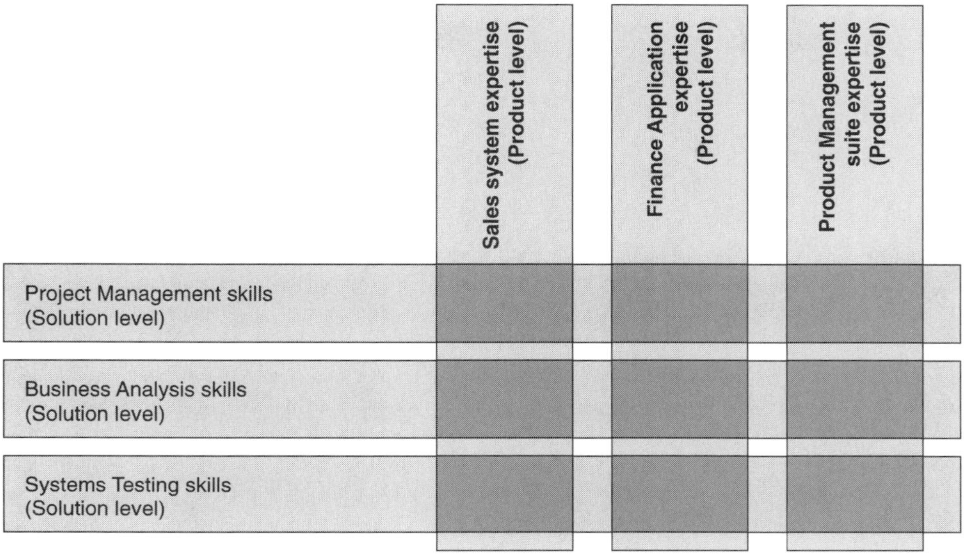

	Sales system expertise (Product level)	Finance Application expertise (Product level)	Product Management suite expertise (Product level)
Project Management skills (Solution level)			
Business Analysis skills (Solution level)			
Systems Testing skills (Solution level)			

Figure 4.4. Solution Delivery – Matrixed

function), what kind of additional technology-independent skills can we bring to bear along the horizontal, i.e. with a focus on the solution and not the individual systems? Business process analysis is one, of course. We have already suggested that this might reside as a function within the service area; however, in some organizations it may be more appropriate to have it resident within a delivery capability. Wherever its 'reporting home' happens to be, it can operate across the three business applications. Additionally, we could look to project management as spanning the solution. Other elements – perhaps in terms of a testing function – might also sit horizontally. Figure 4.4 shows how this might look.

The challenges arise where the groups intersect. In the light grey boxes there are no issues: the Sales system specialists know their software inside and out; the Testing team have a clear generic procedure outlining how all solutions should be tested. It is where the dark boxes occur – the solution/product interfaces – that the IT function will need to be clear on how, internally, the appropriate processes, hand-offs, responsibilities and so forth, reside. One might immediately object to this and argue that if the project management, business analysis and testing skills were resident within the application teams, then the issue goes away. But does it?

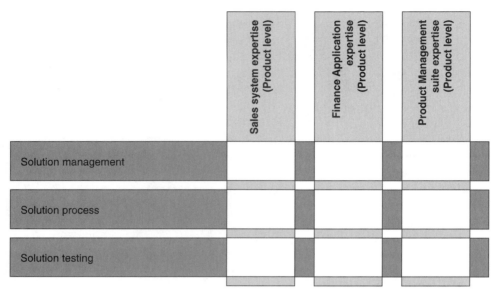

Figure 4.5. Solution Delivery – Non-Matrixed

As Figure 4.5 shows, in placing all the resource within the verticals, the former grey boxes have indeed gone away – however, there are now significant gaps between the specialist areas which, as we have already argued, act as barriers to the successful implementation of solutions, and is the very silo-driven landscape from which we are trying to escape.

However the delivery mechanism might eventually be mapped out in response to a particular need (and there could be many and various ways of doing so), the ultimate measure of IT's performance in this area will be on tangible results, i.e. the delivery of a 'fit for purpose' solution. Unlike the services area where perception plays a large part, the manufacturing function will be judged on 'standard' IT measures:

- Delivery to time
- Delivery to budget
- Delivery in accordance with defined functional requirements
- Meeting quality assurance targets
- Smooth operational introduction, hand-over and live running

Some of these – such as the final point – may well depend on the performance of others outside the delivery function; in this case we might include the trainers from the services area and perhaps the database specialists from operations. This only goes to highlight both the complexity of solutions delivery and the importance of ensuring that, in our new relational organization model, appropriate processes and procedures are in place to ensure that all subfunctions work well together.

4.3.3 Organizational Impact

From a structural perspective, the organizational impact of both solutions and product demands on the delivery function are clear enough. We will never be able to move away from needing specialist resources to support the development of individual technologies, and so a manufacturing function solely comprised of pools of generic resource able to work across any platform and system may be a nirvana that is not achievable. Recognizing that, the issue then becomes making the decision on how close towards this model one is able to go.

There will be a number of critical influencers here, for example:

● How solutions-driven is the business itself? If most of its requirements can be met through discrete systems initiatives (rather than those that span multiple verticals), then taking a largely silo-based approach may be acceptable.

● How dynamic and flexible does the IT function need to be in order to meet the demands that come its way? Even in a legitimate silo-based approach, high degrees of flexibility and responsiveness can reassert the need for more mobile resource pools that can work across the IT estate.

● Where do some of the generic components most logically reside? Does it make sense to retain, for example, the business analysis pool within the services or engagement function? Are there some operational or capability-based skills and technologies – such as database administration or e-mail – which sit more logically within the delivery area?

● How much outsourced delivery is there? As we shall see, this will require special attention from a management perspective, and how this is handled within the delivery function will depend on the degree and mix of outsourced provisioning.

127

Additionally, the IT manager will need to consider exactly what skill-sets he has that can be sensibly pooled. Project Management is one example where, by having a discrete or independent group of resource, allows the development of that resource in a consistent fashion. For example, all project managers could be targeted with gaining Prince accreditation. Mapping out a common and consistent training plan may be less easy if they are working within technology teams where local goals and objectives will take priority. Hopefully the pooling of such resource will lead to consistent processes across all IT projects, whether they are solution- or product-driven.

This consistency of method is perhaps a good measure to judge whether or not a skill-set is suitable to be considered generic and appropriate for a resource pool. We have already suggested a number of areas where the organization may well benefit from having a consistent approach, and not just in the delivery area too: business analysis, testing, training, project office support, database management, disaster recovery/business continuity, quality management (e.g. ISO 9000), internal consultancy, and so on.

One final consideration here is the potential reversal of the product-to-solution trend. It is entirely possible that, even within the delivery environment, some services will need to be "productised" (Brittain and Matlus, 2002). For example, there may have been a significant business demand for a new Internet-based sales solution. This would have included not only the introduction of some new technologies, but also the modification of existing core systems and the introduction of new processes. Such an initiative would have been managed as a solution delivery. However, once the new systems are in and working, the business may regard modifications as simply readjustments of something that is already there, i.e. there are no more solutions to be delivered in this area, and we are in a production line scenario (the original solution having been to build the production line capability in the first place). Questions here for the IT manager will be to decide exactly how to go about this kind of 'operational' requirement for delivery elements. Indeed, is it right to do so within the delivery stream and, if so, how will this effect his organization? Perhaps given an SLA-driven requirement such as this, he might even want to ask the question about transferring responsibility for this delivery into the operations area.

There is a broad question here around commoditization that we should acknowledge. "Even mission-critical services have become commodities, and customisation is giving way to an '80 percent good enough' standardised offerings designed for the shared environment" (Beck, 2002). This has particular relevance in the outsourcing arena, of course, but for an IT function that is attempting to constantly improve its performance and value-add into a business, it must differentiate itself. Becoming a function that is defined – and bound – solely by SLAs will not maximize contribution and could actually lead to a decline in service and effectiveness.

4.4 Operational Management

4.4.1 Keeping The Lights On; Organizational Stability

If the delivery function is about the introduction of change, then one might say that the operational side of the IT organization is about ensuring stability, though obviously this does not mean a strict maintenance of the status quo and a complete absence of change. As we have just seen, there may well be an argument to suggest that some applications, having been passed into a productionized 'steady state', might be handed in to the operations area for ongoing updates or enhancements which are subject to production line SLAs. Indeed, one might even wish to argue that any element of the IT portfolio subject to SLAs might, by default, reside in this area.

Another term used for operations work is 'keeping the lights on' (KTLO) – fundamentally to ensure the ongoing health and performance of those systems and technologies which are already in use. If we choose the e-mail system as an example, not only will this be subject to availability SLAs, there may also be service levels associated with the setting-up and management of mail accounts. Based on our previous argument, we might choose to regard these as production line updates of a steady state system. If so, what do we do when there is a need to upgrade the e-mail software; does the responsibility then shift back into the development area? Undoubtedly not. Upgrades to production systems of this kind should also be regarded as KTLO activity; after all, the work would be undertaken to ensure the ongoing integrity and operability of the system, not in response to any radical new solution implementation.

These types of responsibility – the operational maintenance of the IT estate – are regarded by some as 'utility services'. Many of these 'run the business' investments are allied to core technologies and are effectively non-discretionary. Not completing the e-mail upgrade may, for example, result in violation of licensing agreements, an absence of ongoing maintenance with software vendors, and even – in the most extreme of circumstance – a loss of the service itself. It is around these core technologies that we can argue for the importance of 'capability': the expertise in both specific and generic topics (such as database management) about which we have already spoken.

In many respects this kind of portfolio makes the operations area somewhat easier to cater for from an organizational perspective. Given that the degree of change will be limited yet with a reasonably predictable demand, the associated IT organization may consequently be more solid and/or definitively planned (see The Meta Group, 2002). Indeed, in an environment where reliability and predictability are at a premium, organizational stability is almost a prerequisite.

4.4.2 'Product' Focused; Service-driven

Following our theme in this section of the book, we can argue that our focus in the operations area will, then, be product-based. Unlike the engagement area (which is solutions driven) and delivery (a combination of solution and product), here our KTLO requirements demands operational excellence and a solid capability to support core technologies. This does not mean, as I have said, that there is an exclusion here in terms of making change or contributing to the delivery of new or enhanced systems. Expertise in areas such as capacity planning and disaster recovery, whilst primarily concerned with the portfolio as a whole, will have something essential to add to many development projects or programmes.

Because of the general thrust of responsibility in this area, it is obviously more acceptable to build teams around technologies, i.e. to maintain the 'traditional' way of looking at structure. Examples of cross-vertical expertise will still exist, of course; indeed, capacity planning and disaster recovery may be examples of these, along with topics such as security. However, it is also possible for these to be allied to technologies too. There may be a team within the function whose responsibility is to manage all firewalls within the IT estate. If so, broader aspects of security may be added to their base remit as a kind of 'consultancy extra'. Capacity planning may be a role carried out by specific database or hardware management teams, rather than a generic topic. The difference between these kinds of skills and, say, project management in terms of both generic utilization and resource pooling seems clear enough.

That service is the base measure for the operations area is also an obvious conclusion to be drawn. We have already suggested examples of where SLAs in 'production line' scenarios might apply. There are some additional challenges which perhaps impact more here than elsewhere, even though they are not unique to operations. It is, for example, highly unlikely that all core technologies will be delivered in-house. Take provision of Internet access. This will be a utility service provided by the operations function to its business customers as a core technology managed under SLA; however, much of the service may be provided externally, through a telecommunications or Internet specialist. Operations' SLA will be impacted if there is a problem with the service provider, and such dependence places an additional management overhead on the function. Of course, external suppliers may assist in other functional areas too – such as specialist consultants in software development – but the critical difference is that performance measures for operations are likely to be absolutely specific.

I suggested earlier that the presence of an SLA might prove to be a useful guide in terms of defining the responsibility location for particular technologies. If this seems reasonable enough, we will need to keep in mind that some operational capabilities – perhaps security management – may not fall easily into this category. After all, there will be a key element of KTLO activity that is about prevention of incidents rather than maintenance of a particular level of service. Thus, as with all things, we must acknowledge exceptions to generic rules.

4.4.3 Organizational Impact

Given all that we have said with respect to the operations function, it seems reasonable to assert that, organizationally, there are likely to be fewer difficulties here than elsewhere. Teams based around core technologies driven by a capability requirement and service need would seem to be the order of the day. In terms of structural components then, we might wish to draw up a list that contains the following kinds of activity:

● Hardware operation and management (by platform)

● Software operating systems and management (by technology)

- Database systems and management (by technology)
- Network and communications management
- Business continuity and disaster recovery
- Capacity planning
- Change and release management

Some of these will be 'small' roles (in terms of resource numbers) that may potentially impact all technology groupings; change management is an example. In cases such as this, the role of the change management function will be to provide procedural assurance in an area that will apply across multiple teams, i.e. formal change control should exist in both hardware and software areas to ensure continuity of service before, during and after critical upgrade work.

There are two other areas I would like to single out for final comment: application support and the help desk. In many organizations support for live applications remains within the development area, i.e. with the teams responsible for initial implementations. This is perfectly fine. There may, however, be times when – as I have already suggested – the support required is so fundamentally procedural and SLA-driven, that it can be regarded as operational KTLO work. These examples may not be the norm, but the IT manager should not shy away from locating this kind of activity within the operational environment simply because it is an 'application'. Remember, the definitions of 'delivery' and 'operations' we are working to here are subtly different from that which might be seen as traditional.

In the case of the help desk function, how this is resourced and organized will very much depend on the remit of the function. Is it, for example, simply a call-handling operation or is it charged with first- or even second-line fixes? Is the help desk 'static', or does it have people whose job is to go and 'visit' customers at their working location in order to resolve problems? How these questions are answered will change the organization's shape accordingly. Of course, however it is defined, there will need to be solid procedures in place linking the help desk not only with other operations teams, but also into the delivery and engagement areas too.

The other major factor that will effect the way a help desk is resourced – and, to an extent, some of the other operations functions too – will be the period of cover required by the business. If the commercial operation is international or 'round the clock', then there will be a need to provide appropriate technical cover twenty-four hours per day, seven days a week. Manning any function on a 24×7 basis can be a logistical headache. For example, it is suggested that even for a modest 24×7 operation a minimum of ten people will be required. Not only this, but you will need to ensure that all relevant skill-sets are available during the period too, so it may rapidly become more than just a numbers game. This consideration does not change the fundamentals of the organizational shape, but is obviously a significant consideration in the final picture.

4.5 Delivering Performance and Value

However the solutions–products amalgam is mixed, the ultimate drivers for the IT manager in delivering his service to the business will be the same, i.e. delivering performance and value. As we have seen, how these are articulated will vary from element to element; the IT manager will need to be able to bundle these measures together in such a way as to define how he and his function have performed.

You may think that the split into products and solutions – and then the further decomposition within these groupings at project level – makes it harder to provide an overview that would offer a score card for the whole department. There may indeed be a little extra work required in normalizing the input from various programmes and work streams, however such an atomic breakdown does actually improve the manageability of each, and in particular the key components against which metrics will be taken: delivery (time, functionality and service) and resource (people and money). Not only that, being able to reduce systems initiatives to this fundamental level may help the manager to not only articulate issues, but also secure additional resource.

For example, the spend on a particular system offers a service level availability of 97% and a turnaround time for changes of 5 days; however, for the business, this is proving inadequate. The IT manager should be able to offer alternative spend–performance equations; perhaps spending an extra 5% on the system (additional resource, extra hardware, and so on) may move availability to 97.5% and reduce turnaround by half a day; 10% may take the system to 98% and 4 days. Being able to report and articulate performance in this way may therefore serve two purposes:

primarily the reporting itself, but also business case support should it be needed.

Reporting on both solutions and products will be essential therefore in articulating performance, and the IT manager should aim for at least the following:

- For each solution:
  - Budget, estimate and actual (absolute and percentage)
  - Delivery against milestones, percentages early, on-time and late
  - Resource in man days effort, estimate and actual (absolute and percentage)

- For each product:
  - Service, target SLA against actual performance
  - Budget, estimate and actual (absolute and percentage)
  - Delivery against milestones, percentages early, on-time and late (if appropriate)
  - Work-stack status; numbers of open jobs, turnaround time, etc.
  - Resource in man days effort, estimate and actual (absolute and percentage)

In order to facilitate this more easily, there should be a standard set of metrics across all solutions and products and a consistent method for calculating and presenting the results. If this is not the case, how else will the IT manager be able to decide where he might place additional resource to best effect?

Of course, reporting against solutions and products in this way is just one part of the performance articulation equation. The second element – which begins to stray into the 'value-add' area – concerns trends over time; this is obviously another significant reason to have standard and repeatable reporting processes. Trend reporting will take a similar format as above and will, of course, be based on the same data. However, in the solutions area, we may be reporting against generic rather than specific trends because the compositions of projects and programmes will vary over time; how can you report a meaningful performance trend on a project that lasts only two months? On this basis, I would advocate something along these lines:

- For each major solution (i.e. consisting of a number of programmes/ projects and running in excess of one year):
  - Budget, estimate and actual (percentage trend)
  - Delivery against milestones, percentage trends (early, on-time and late)
  - Resource in man days effort, estimate and actual (percentage trend)
- For all other solutions, work as a single 'pot':
  - Budget, estimate and actual (percentage trend)
  - Delivery against milestones, percentage trends (early, on-time and late)
  - Resource in man days effort, estimate and actual (percentage trend)
- For each significant product (e.g. e-mail, automated backup):
  - Service, target SLA against actual performance (trend)
  - Budget, estimate and actual (percentage trend)
  - Delivery against milestones, percentage trends early, on-time and late (if appropriate)
  - Work-stack status; numbers of open jobs, turnaround time, etc. (as absolute trend)
  - Resource in man days effort, estimate and actual (percentage trend)
- For all remaining products, a consolidated report:
  - Budget, estimate and actual (percentage trend)
  - Delivery against milestones, percentage trends early, on-time and late (if appropriate)
  - Resource in man days effort, estimate and actual (percentage trend)
- Globally (i.e. for the entire function):
  - Budget, estimate and actual (percentage trend)
  - Headcount, estimate and actual (percentage trend)
  - Staff attrition, customer satisfaction, etc. (all as percentage trends)

Moreover, I would advocate that these trend reports be shown in graphical form rather than using raw data. In this way a picture can be established very easily – in which direction is the trend line going, up or down? – without the need to get embroiled in the detail.

We should have now reached the point where the IT manager can demonstrate a) what his teams are working on, b) how those initiatives are performing, and c) significant trends over time. This addresses performance aspects and, to a degree, value-add, i.e. the IT manager should be able to demonstrate that the extra 5% he received to invest in improving the SLA and turnaround time on that system did actually result in achieving the targets set. Of course the area that is harder to articulate in terms of value-add is the delivery of business benefit gained from IT investments, fundamentally because in the majority of instances it is not IT's responsibility to realize those benefits. I do not propose to go into further detail here other than to say that the IT manager should endeavour to find a way of getting his customers to both realize and then articulate the benefits they gain from the delivery of IT solutions. Additionally some organizations may gain from establishing a 'benefits management' function within the 'services' area; this would be a function working hand-in-hand with both the business and engagement/ programme managers to help IT's customers to deliver the full range of promised solution benefits. (This is a role that can, in the vast majority of cases, sit with the engagement or programme manager, and be addressed throughout the project as well as more formally during any post-implementation review.)

One thing that an effective reporting regimen can provide the IT manager and his customers is a clear indication of solutions or products which may prove to be – or are! – too expensive. Perhaps for the money being invested it is felt that the achievable SLA is inadequate; perhaps, despite a particular level of resource investment, the delivery of one or more solutions is not felt to meet desired business timetables. In these kinds of instance, the IT manager might have effective arguments either for – or against – other provisioning alternatives, primarily outsourcing. However, a final word here; even when solutions delivery or product capability is outsourced to third parties, the reporting schema employed internally by the IT manager must still apply; it is the only way to ensure that like-for-like comparisons can be made, and the only way to judge those external provisioning organizations in the same way as the internal function. Indeed, at the end of the day, the business will want to see the overall picture for the IT organization, whoever is supplying the service.

Outsourcing

5

5.1 Introduction

5.1.1 The Growth in Outsourcing

In many circumstances over the past few years decisions on systems provisioning options have become increasingly difficult in parallel with the overall IT landscape gaining in complexity. Not only that, demands on IT functions have grown in terms of volume of requests, with a greater emphasis on speed and flexibility of delivery. Very often, all of these factors combine with commercial pressures on IT managers to 'do more with less'. For many this has led to a gap emerging between what can be provisioned locally and that which is needed by the business; a gap that can represent a shortfall in effort, time, skills or any of the micro components of the systems delivery process.

In Figure 5.1 we can see how the compound expansion of delivery pressures from elements such as complexity, speed and workload can easily outstrip an overall capability, even if this has also grown over time.

This picture has undoubtedly been made more complex by a change in the commercial world (from a systems perspective) within which enterprises now operate. Business models are shifting in relation to pressures from the market; it is not just a question of wanting more of the same things more quickly, new things are now wanted in addition. Provision of Internet systems is an obvious example here, as is the move towards solutions implementation rather than the more straightforward product delivery. For people like Da Rold (2001), it is critical to recognize both the gap between capability and business objective at the corporate level, and how this is tackled: "the sourcing strategy should build a bridge between the enterprise's current status and capabilities and the desired future ability to fulfil business objectives" (Da Rold, 2001).

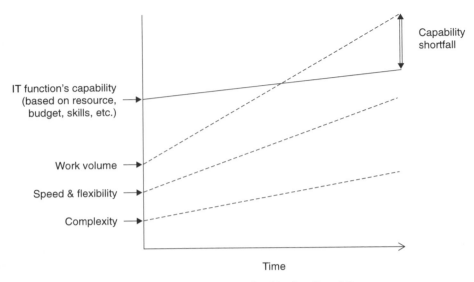

IT function's capability (based on resource, budget, skills, etc.)

Work volume

Speed & flexibility

Complexity

Capability shortfall

Time

Figure 5.1. *The Systems Provisioning Shortfall*

Relevant at the overall company level, we can apply this theory with some validity to the IT function within it. Da Rold suggests a simple Boston matrix to help businesses [sic, IT functions] analyse where they are located prior to defining their strategic sourcing strategy (see Figure 5.2). In each segment, Da Rold estimates the percentage occupancy by the business community at large and, I suggest, these figures might not be that far out for IT functions too.

- 'Beginner' – This represents the 40% or so of organizations whose IT strategy is either poorly defined or not defined at all, or where, even if it were, the IT function would be poorly placed to execute against that strategy.

- 'Visionary' – The strategy is more or less in place, but the function is unable to execute it.

- 'Challenger' – Here the IT function is well placed to execute against any given strategy; the problem is that it does not have one, or the one it does have is inadequate.

- 'Master' – That minority of IT organizations (5%?) that not only have a strategy, but are also capable of delivering against it.

It is clear that in each of these segments the systems provisioning strategy will differ. In this chapter I aim to take a look at outsourcing: why do

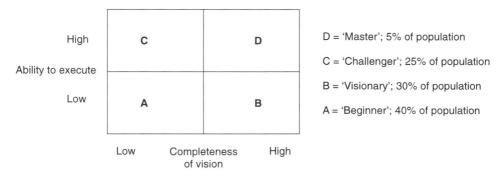

Figure 5.2. *Vision vs. Execution Ability*

we do it, and what impact does it have on the 'internal' or customer IT organization? How do we ensure the management of outsourced services, and what needs to be done internally to enable this? And what about risk? How much of outsourcing is about sharing risk – and how much outsourcing actually results in unwittingly increasing it? Structurally, what can the IT manager do to mitigate against this?

5.1.2 Reasons for Outsourcing

We have already begun to identify why companies pursue an outsourcing strategy for some (if not all) of their IT capability. Indeed, based on the Boston matrix in Figure 5.2, it would be easy to see why 'Beginners' or 'Visionaries' might wish to go down this route. Analysts such as Diromualdo (1998) suggest three primary reasons for outsourcing: i) IT improvement; ii) improved business performance and/or impact; and iii) commercial gain. We will look at each of these in turn.

IT Improvement

So what might we include in the notion of 'IT improvement'? Quite clearly any idea of making tangible gains in this area must equate to an increase in systems performance. Given our recent discussion in Chapter 4, we could specifically target a number of key areas – already identified as critical performance metrics – where outsourcing might be pursued with a view to enhancing contribution:

● Service – targeting SLA improvements
● Budget – 'doing more for less'

139

- Delivery – being able to perform more consistently against milestones, with fewer being missed

- Work-stack status – reducing the numbers of open jobs and cutting turnaround time

From the simple chart (Figure 5.1) showing the underlying problem, we might also choose to argue that one could also outsource to address the 'capability shortfall' that may have grown over time. In addition to tackling potential resourcing issues (which, if simply recruiting contract staff, would not strictly constitute outsourcing), the strategy could be adopted to meet shortfalls in other areas:

- Expertise – where an internal function simply does not have a particular capability

- Speed/Flexibility – where an external supplier can actually perform the same function as the internal team, but can do it more rapidly or be more open to rapid change

- Cost – because it is cheaper

These kinds of decisions would most probably be made locally, i.e. at the discretion of the IT manager and supported by appropriate business cases. But where would one go to identify potential outsourcing opportunities? We have already discussed a number of possible tools to assist here. For example, an application alignment exercise following a portfolio management cycle "can help clarify what capabilities to buy off the shelf and what to build in-house, and identify areas and functions that might be well suited to outsourcing" (Barton, 2002). Indeed, Barton's own Boston matrix outlining strategic value against operational importance (Figure 3.1) may help us further here. For example, some IT managers would strongly resist outsourcing anything that was either of the highest strategic or of operational importance.

Improved Business Performance/Impact

If IT improvement is about local parochial gains, then to a degree outsourcing motives around business performance or impact could be seen as being independent of the IT function itself. Before moving on, perhaps I should clarify the definition of outsourcing to which I am working. For me outsourcing is 'the sub-contracting of IT provisioning responsibility for a specific and pre-defined technological deliverable, solution or product'; this would encompass, for example, provision of a help desk function, off-site support for a payroll application, or the delivery of an Internet presence.

In terms of where outsourcing might be adopted with a business (and not IT) focus, we might consider examples such as collaborative e-business solutions where a third party provides an extranet-type facility for a cartel of related businesses, and where this solution includes running all associated hardware and software on behalf of the members of that community. Although this is an example of a business-driven outsourcing arrangement, it is still relevant to the IT manager because a) there may well be interfaces to and from local core systems, and b) even if there are not, the business will probably expect IT to manage the outsourcing relationship.

Commercial Gain

The third outsourcing category is around financial reward. Here the argument follows that, although it may be possible to provide a particular service from within the local IT function, it may prove cheaper to buy in that same function from elsewhere. This may be true not only in absolute terms, but can also be adopted if one is in a 'pilot' phase, i.e. uncertain as to whether or not a specific service/technology is going to be adopted; a short-term outsourcing arrangement can be undertaken to establish the viability of the project (rather than the means of provision).

Of course the notion of outsourcing for commercial gain can, for some businesses, become incredibly broad. Rather than talking about outsourcing for particular projects or products, some companies have outsourced their entire IT capability, retaining few in-house IT staff – and these primarily managers to look after the third-party suppliers. This kind of arrangement is most often pursued as an extreme 'do more with less' philosophy, with senior executives being lured by promises of multi-million-dollar savings against their traditional IT budgets. Whether these promises are actually met or not will vary of course, although I suspect there are likely to be more managing directors who find themselves financially disappointed than otherwise.

5.1.3 Challenges for the Customer's IT Organization

One of the dangers lying in wait for the IT manager who either undertakes or in some way inherits an outsourcing arrangement, is to assume that it will have no significant impact on his organization. After all, surely outsourcing is just a different group of people doing something that, given the appropriate skills and resource, he could do himself? Surely it is just an extension of his overall IT team? At a superficial level this is true, however in adopting this stance one is choosing to ignore the fact that the outsourcing partner is ultimately working to an agenda that differs from that of their customers, i.e. they are primarily in business to make a profit and gain commercially, not to satisfy every customer's whim at whatever cost to themselves. For Dreyfuss (2002), "although many enterprises are moving toward a multi-sourced environment, they fail to realize that the traditional organization and traditional management practices are not appropriate to manage it".

When considering the way in which the IT manager articulates the performance of his function, I suggested that whatever reporting format or mechanism is put in place, any outsourcing partner should be 'encouraged' to conform to that same model. Indeed, it should be a requirement of the contract. However, it would be a mistake to think that just getting numbers reported in the same way automatically gave one control over the service being provided. I would also argue that adding the responsibility for managing an outsourced help desk to the operations manager's remit as another element of the 'day job' is also going to guarantee nothing. Such an arrangement is unlikely to have the required result because a) the operations manager is probably busy enough already, and b) they will almost certainly apply the same kind of management technique and style to the outsourcing partner as they use with their own internal teams.

Managing an outsourcing supplier is a different problem altogether. If asking internal teams to do something extra or make that additional effort, they are likely to comply because they are part of the organization, have company loyalties, know their efforts will be recognized at pay review time, and so on. For an outsourcer, there is the possibility that such a request will immediately result in changes in costs or timescales. Perhaps there is an outsourced development arrangement with a software vendor where the customer organization purchases twenty-five days' programming effort per month. As soon as a request is logged for the twenty-sixth day's effort, an invoice is raised. Because this is the kind of thing that would not happen internally, it demands a different kind of management and a different kind of focus. My argument is, therefore, that in an environment when outsourcing is part of the IT landscape, the role of outsource supplier manager should be recognized and, if appropriate, should be allocated to dedicated resources.

Another mistake that is commonly made with outsourcing is that the IT manager can turn a blind eye to the capability he is buying; by this I mean that, knowing he is hiring in the skill-set needed, he assumes that he can cease to be concerned about not having that skill-set within his own team. The arguments that "an organization should not use external capabilities just because it cannot reach an objective with its internal capabilities" (Da Rold, 2002), and that you should "make sure your organization and the outsourcing vendor have the right mix of competencies and know-how" (Diromualdo, 1998) are complimentary. It may be that, even if you do not have the skills you need, the 'right' answer to your problem may be to build the capability internally rather than go outside; immediately making an outsourcing assumption may be incorrect. And even when you do utilize a third party, it can be essential to ensure that you have some measure of capability internally; what happens, for example, when the outsourcing partner you have relied on to support your financial system suddenly goes out of business and you have no-one internally who can hold the fort for a short period?

Not only this, some third parties will promise anything and make unrealistic claims about their capabilities in order to secure your business. One area where this is common is where outsourcers laud the capabilities of their staff, and then – once they have your business – they simply go to the contract resource market and recruit the very same people that you could have hired yourself. Recognition that "it is not sufficient simply to accept vendor claims of capabilities" (Diromualdo, 1998) is an argument not only to ensure that you retain or build some knowledge internally, but also advocates the unique nature of the outsourcing management role. If there is not someone specifically focused on getting the correct outsourcing deal – and who will be measured on its ongoing performance in the live environment – then your recruitment of partners could become dangerously amateurish. For Diromualdo (1998), "the most effective approach [is] focused on jointly developing complementary skills and capabilities, rather than simply relying on those of the vendor"; this has to be sound advice.

One final thought; for many new to the concept, outsourcing will be something of a 'leap of faith'. They may be concerned about whether or not it will work, how to manage it, and so forth. One of the obvious solutions to address some of these concerns may be to consider only the larger, more obvious outsourcing partners; after all, the argument might go, they have been in the business for a long time and they know what they are doing. Undoubtedly true. However, because of this they may also be 'slicker' when it comes to their own processes; they may have a way of working which you cannot influence; they may be inflexible in some way; they will certainly be wiser than you; and, at the end of the day, they may not care that much about you as an individual customer. The advice of Foote et al. (2001) to "include strange bedfellows" is worth keeping in mind. Perhaps that small company does not appear to have the track record even if they do have the skills – but if you partner with them are you not likely to be very important to them, their success being tied in with your own? Is it not possible that this will give you a greater degree of influence over the relationship? Might they not go the extra mile for you? And it may be that the skills you need reside outside of the 'normal' IT arena too. If you need to outsource web development expertise, perhaps this may exist in spades in a non-IT graphics or design company who would jump at the chance to work for you – and at a considerably lower cost. Again, all of these considerations point to the fact that your organization will need to support any outsourcing arrangement – proposed or actual – effectively and professionally.

5.2 Service Management

5.2.1 Outsourcing for Service Delivery

Perhaps the most common use of outsourcing is for the delivery of a specific service, irrespective of whether the motivation is for IT improvement, business impact or financial gain. In many respects service delivery outsourcing is not that new; in the 1970s and 1980s there were organizations who offered 'bureaux' services to their customers where the customer paid for a specific IT-driven service; perhaps running a payroll system or the utilization of specialist niche players in the technology market – EDI (electronic data interchange) for example. Where modern-day outsourcing differs is in that the supplier takes on a greater degree of responsibility for the service, offering more of a complete, bundled and 'ring-fenced' package. These kinds of utility services are gaining in popularity; in exchange for a pre-defined fee, you will receive a pre-agreed service. Perhaps the distinction between these and bureaux services is a subtle one, but there is certainly more to outsourcing – "service co-ordination, sourcing and evaluation" (Dreyfuss, 2002) – than simply agreeing on a partner.

In the delivery of capability through external agencies, the part that the service level agreement (SLA) has to play is absolutely key; it is the requirement by which the original commercial terms are agreed, and it is the yardstick by which the performance of the supplier is measured. What kinds of things from a typical IT estate might be outsourced in order to provide benefit to the IT function or business as a whole?

- On-site/remote help desk. Here the supplier provides an initial point of contact for all day-to-day problems and queries in relation to overall systems provision. SLAs are likely to revolve around call volumes, response times, customer satisfaction and first-line fix rates.

- Internet connectivity and web presence. In this case the service provided would be measured on Internet availability locally, response times and fault calls. With both this and the help desk service, process interfaces into any in-house back-office systems will need to be clearly defined and agreed in order to prevent disputes arising over any failure to meet SLAs.

- Application development. This is the provision and support of a business application (which may be software alone, or both hardware and software). In these kinds of arrangements, performance SLAs can be harder to measure. Some elements – such as numbers of man-days available and fault rates – are easy enough to monitor, but others based around delivering the required functionality can be much tougher to define.

Whatever the service, it is absolutely essential that both parties are clear up-front as to the basics of the deal – and in particular the concrete numbers involved in the SLAs, associated costs/resource equations, and any penalties for underachieving.

5.2.2 Key Success Elements

It would be all too easy to draw up a simple equation that asserted 'delivery of SLA equals outsourcing success' and leave it at that. For many, such a superficial metric is sufficient in terms of both performance measurement and justification of approach. However, we must recognize that achieving an SLA of 87% against a target of 85% does not necessarily mean that the outsourcing arrangement is working; recall that earlier I offered the example of an e-mail SLA that was being hit and yet its users thought the service was terrible.

For Diromualdo (1998), "success factors are more business oriented than technical". This might seem an odd statement to make when I have

145

defined the metrics of outsourcing as being in areas where 'technical' measurement is practical: service, budget, delivery, work-stack status, and resource effort. However, there will be additional considerations which may prove to be less 'black and white', and it might be these that will settle the evaluation of success in the final analysis.

So what are these other factors? Not surprisingly, given the general thrust of some of the arguments we have pursued thus far, they reside more in engagement and management. Consider the following suggestions; if there were difficulties in these areas would you still be prepared to stamp the outsourcing arrangement with your approval?

- Supplier engagement. There are a number of areas in which relationships with the supplier could be troublesome: Are they inflexible in terms of their reporting or process? Do they insist on completion of the minutiae of detail in terms of paperwork for even the smallest request? Do they need to be chased to provide routine information or updates? Do they charge for everything?

- Personnel. How the supplier's staff engages with those of the customer – at all levels – will be key. There may be issues if, as a result of inflexibility elsewhere, they refuse to engage under certain circumstances, thereby being seen as unhelpful. Problems with individuals – such as lateness, rudeness, inappropriate behaviour, etc. – can be more readily dealt with if they are an internal employee. How does the third party respond if there are such issues with their people?

- Management overhead. Some outsourcers may require a considerable degree of management overhead. This can arise for a number of reasons. In addition to the two above, is there a constant need to be checking up on them to ensure they are doing what they said they would? Do you feel the need to get involved to help them resolve the problems they patently have, and which they cannot resolve themselves?

Your partner may hit all the SLAs you have agreed with them, but failure in the areas above and – more significantly – your inability to manage those failures, can negate all the good work that may be being done.

The engagement needs to work on another level too. For example, "relationships with the vendor … must be aligned with the strategic intent underlying the outsourcing initiative" (Diromualdo, 1998), i.e. what they do and how they do it must align with your overall objective as the customer. Some problems in this area can be placed firmly at your door as client; for example, pursuing cost reduction measures through outsourcing could be counter-productive where the achievement of the ultimate objective may require a creative or innovative solution, i.e. not something bound by cost. This would be a failure on the customer's part to outsource the right things. Where there might also be an issue is in strategic alignment where the outsourcer's own strategy – perhaps in terms of technology or product development – differs from the customer's. I wrote earlier of the need to recognize the unique agenda the supplier will have as an independent commercial entity; what if this gets in the way? Perhaps you are buying a fully managed outsourced ERP solution and you become aware that a new module has been made available by the software supplier. This module may fit perfectly with your business strategy, and you could get real benefit from its rapid introduction. But what if the outsourcer has no plans to introduce the new software for another six months for reasons of his own?

There is a broader generic point here which, for Beck (2002), is summed up in the fact that "vendors are still not delivering on the promise of technology nor are they clearly able to articulate their real value-add". Just like IT managers, outsourcers face the same challenges to prove value and contribution, and to continually improve. If they are not doing so, or – perhaps even more significantly – if they are not living up to promises made, all the achieved SLAs in the world may not redress something that could be seen as a significant shortfall. We assume that the fault here will lie with the outsourcer, but this is not necessarily the case. What if the customer has failed to engage them properly, or neglected to keep them up-to-date with their needs, thoughts and developments?

5.2.3 Organizing IT to Manage the Outsourced Service

It seems clear that there is a need to endorse the customer–outsourcer relationship with the same emphasis on focus and alignment as we have already suggested be applied to IT's internal customers. For outsourced provisioning the alignment is similar: firstly it is with the individual outsourcers, and secondly, it could be through a logical grouping of the services delivered through these third parties.

Let us assume that an IT function has four outsourcing contracts:

- For a Help Desk function which is provided off-site at the outsourcer's own premises, and which acts as the 'front line' to the IT function.

147

- For a Desktop Support function that exists as a team of people who reside within the parent IT function, and whose role is to manage a consistent and functioning desktop environment. This also includes second-line fix (first-line being with the help desk via the telephone).

- For a Human Resources and Payroll application. This is run and managed on hardware and software located off-site, but which is accessed through a standard desktop icon as if it were a local application.

- For Internet access and capability, including a small marketing-focused site aimed at external customers.

How might we align with these initiatives?

As the first two of these contracts sit firmly within the operations area – and as there is a clear link between help desk and desktop support – it would seem to make sense to have an outsourcing manager responsible for the maintenance of these services. Co-locating responsibility in the same individual will help to ensure processes that link them (i.e. first- to second-line support) are working effectively. The HR and Payroll application, although obviously a development-type activity, may sit quite isolated in the IT portfolio. By this I mean that a finance system would, if outsourced, still need to interface with many other systems that may be managed locally or via a number of other outsource contracts. Our HR and Payroll system may be stand-alone in this regard – so much so, that there may only be one person within the IT team who has any real interest in it. This could, therefore, be a management role for a single individual; or, if this was not warranted in terms of size, the responsibility could be allocated as an additional charge to another delivery or outsourcing manager. One needs to be careful here because there is a danger of both loss of focus and lack of rigour if the responsibility is seen as a 'minor' part of someone's job. The Internet outsourcing arrangement is, as so often the case, a mix of both operations and development: technological access and business application. On this basis it could be valid to consider locating the responsibility within either operations or development, depending on the size and bias of the service delivered. Whichever was felt most appropriate, again the message is that there needs to be a single manager who 'owns' delivery of the service.

Before moving on, we need to cover two key generic questions: exactly what is the role of the outsourcing manager and where do business customers fit in? In answering the second question first, we can say that the role and commitment of the business should be exactly the same as if it were an internal team that was providing the service. In the case of both help desk and desktop support we can say (for now) that the IT function is itself the customer, but for the other two systems there will need to be key users in both HR and Marketing functions who take ownership of the business activity and process from a non-technical perspective. Thus we build an identical relationship as already outlined for the engagement manager. Indeed, an outsourcing manager is almost a dual engagement manager in some instances; their interfaces go 'out' to the outsourcing organization and 'in' to the business unit with which the service is aligned.

As for the role of the outsourcing manager, we might suggest that its primary objective is delivery of the service. This is a fundamental notion. I have not said that their remit is to manage the outsourcer to deliver the service; this removes the outsourcing manager from ultimate responsibility by a step, which in turn can weaken the quality of the service provided. My suggestion is that it is the outsourcing manager who is responsible for hitting the SLAs, and the third party is the mechanism at their disposal to do so. This gives the manager some 'skin in the game'; not only that, it means that they will need to be proactive and driving, and must engage in such a way as to be able to deal with (i.e. remove) the kinds of issues we outlined earlier. It also suggests that the role is truly a significant one if it is going to be undertaken correctly – which brings me back to my suggestion that simply giving the responsibility to a manager who is already over-burdened is likely to lead to failure.

5.3 Risk Management

5.3.1 Outsourcing for Risk Management

There is another reason in addition to those already considered – service, budget, delivery, etc. – that can be a primary motivator for entering into IT outsourcing deals: the management of risk. For applications and systems residing within the bailiwick of an internal IT function, the risk associated with those technologies is co-located with them. Thus, if there is a problem with the sales order system which means it is off-line for a number of days resulting in the loss of £10,000 worth of orders, then the business bears this risk itself. With the rise in the trend to outsource, businesses are beginning to look to these contracts as a means to manage or mitigate such risk. Put simply, the logic suggests that if the sales order system was an outsourced system and service was interrupted, the

£10,000 of lost orders would result in contractually-driven compensation to the same amount from the outsourcer to the customer organization, i.e. there might be no financial loss at all because the supplier was bearing the risk. This notion that "solutions providers ... assume risks normally borne by the customer" (Foote et al., 2001) can extend beyond service SLAs (as in the sales order system) through to budgetary and manpower considerations too. Indeed, for many executives, the notion of outsourcing the majority of IT functions – which not only removes a headache (because they do not understand it, or it is not performing) but also takes risk with it – is a compelling proposition. Who would not be attracted by a promise of a known service at a known cost and with no risks attached? In fact, at the 'global' level of outsourcing, "risks deal with organizational performance: the solutions provider guarantees that many parts of many different organizations will work together effectively" (Foote et al., 2001) – or many parts of the same organization. Potentially the outsourcer can even encroach on core elements of business process, thereby 'taking away' additional risk residing outside of the IT function.

If it were that simple everyone would outsource everything of course – perhaps even leading to outsourcers subcontracting some their core competencies too. Logically the whole notion could spiral out of control, with the initial customer having no idea who his actual service provider was and consequently no control over them either. In asserting that this is not the norm and that it is never likely to become so, it would be useful to consider what outsourcing risk transference actually implies.

Figure 5.3, based on a proposition by Da Rold (2002), depicts a risk transference model where, in travelling between full internal delivery and entirely outsourced service provision, we can see not only the impact on the 'amount' of risk transferred but also implied changes to the internal management workload. Da Rold suggests six stages of sourcing capabilities or deliverables:

1. Staff augmentation. In adding skill-sets into an already existing framework, this "tends to be very technically oriented and does not imply risk transfer outside the client organization". If anything the management overhead actually rises slightly.

2. Management capability. Here the augmentation includes the transference of a degree of programme management, an approach that "starts by transferring a small part of the risk from the client to an external provider" and reduces some internal management workload.

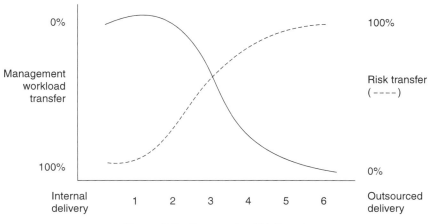

Figure 5.3. Outsourcing Risk Transfer

3. Entire projects. This is where an outsourcer would take entire responsibility for an individual project, including all management, resourcing and budgets.

4. Application Service Provision (ASP). This kind of total, 'bundled' outsource solution is "a very compelling proposition to the client", offering an agreed service level for a known cost – particularly as "up to 90 percent of the IT risk and management workload is transferred to the provider".

5. Business process operation. Here the outsourcer goes beyond the ASP model and enhances their offering by managing internal business processes. Effectively this means handing over the running of some core business element to an external company.

6. Create, buy, partner, merge. The logical next step after step 5 – although this actually leads to a larger corporate entity and potentially the beginning of the cycle all over again. If a business subcontracts all its IT needs to a single third party and then buys that third-party organization, it only succeeds in 're-internalizing' that which it sought to outsource in the first place.

The vast majority of outsourcing deals – and those with which we are primarily concerned here – reside around stages 2, 3 and 4. Once we get to options 5 and 6, we are dealing in a completely different word of business practice.

As you can see, the further we travel towards the right of the chart, the greater the volume of risk that is theoretically transferred out of the business. In parallel with this, more and more of the associated management activity is transferred with it. There is one core implication here for me in this very useful analysis, and it is simply this: transfer risk, lose control.

5.3.2 Some Key Factors

In addition to the organizational elements we have recently discussed, there are some significant considerations here for the business or IT manager who is looking to outsource elements of their service provision. Management questions arise at each of those key stages we are concerned with from the list outlined above – as well as some generic issues:

- Management capability. In outsourcing programme management responsibilities – perhaps allied to an element of resource provision – the IT manager will need to ensure that there is absolute clarity in the remit of the external programme manager. For example, if one of the major consultancies is given the responsibility to implement a new customer management system utilizing a mix of their own and internal IT staff, there will be a need for an explicit understanding in terms of how far that programme manager can go in terms of resource utilization. Exactly what can they approve or sign-off financially? What responsibility do they have for the internal staff working on the project? Will there be a need for any additional management reporting from the programme because they are an external supplier (perhaps additional SLAs), or are they subject to the same rules – and given the same allowances – as an internal programme manager? If something goes awry, where will the responsibility for this lie? Fundamentally, these are basic questions around what and how the outsourcers manage.

- Entire projects. For entire projects, many of the questions raised above will need to be answered; clarity around sign-off, management scope and decision-making are all echoed here. There may also be a need for a different type of engagement from the internal IT manager too. In the programme management example, having some internal resource working on the project actually helps from the perspective of visibility and understanding. If the project is effectively a 'closed shop', how formal interfaces are conducted at the management level will be critical. Similarly critical will be any relationships with the business community. It is all too easy in these types of project for the outsourcing team to engage the business users so effectively that the IT function is cut out of the equation. This can result in decisions being taken for the benefit of the project which may compromise other elements of the IT estate.

● Application Service Provision (ASP). As we move further along the outsourcing axis, we find that management impact could multiply further, i.e. including both sets of considerations from management capability and entire projects. In fact, I would suggest that, although the management overhead falls from a day-to-day perspective (Da Rold's argument), there is an increase in a new type of management, i.e. that at the overall outsourcer level. This is only logical in the example of an ASP service. If, for example, an IT function were providing a help desk internally, it would have direct control over all resources (people, budget, hardware, software) which, when combined, went to make up achievement of the SLA. With an outsourced help desk, those base SLAs remain, but the immediacy of management for the customer IT function is removed; this must mean that we need to introduce some form of 'new' management that was previously absent.

I would like to push my last argument a little further in suggesting that the notion of outsourcing to enable some kind of magical risk-transference is self-deluding. In the case of the failing sales order system we quoted earlier, if it was outsourced and there is a failure then, certainly, there may be financial compensation to the notional value of the orders lost. But the impact may be greater and longer term. Perhaps the customers who could not place their orders due to the loss of service now choose to take their business to our competitors; the £10,000 then compounds to become a much greater figure. The outsourcer would not recompense for that loss and so the risk transference would not be total. Indeed, how can it be? If there is a problem with the service provided by an outsourced supplier, then ultimately it will be the customer's business that must surely suffer. When we buy products from an electrical store, although they do not make the goods themselves, if we continually have problems with quality and performance might we not choose to shop elsewhere?

As with the notion of 'new' management, the further we travel towards completely outsourced services so we introduce 'new' risks that were not there before. One reason for this is becoming managementally myopic, i.e. because we have outsourced we assume all will be fine and take the service provisioning for granted: "the risk is that organizations use external providers to carry out important business initiatives

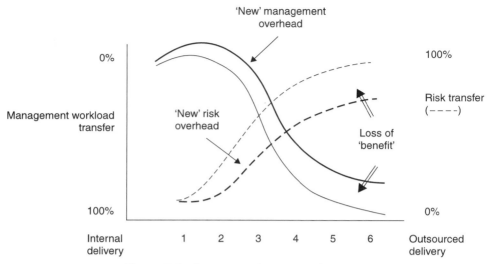

Figure 5.4. *Outsourcing Risk Transfer (Revised)*

without building enough internal capabilities. This results in systems and solutions that are sub-optimal or even disconnected from the current organization and business needs" (Da Rold, 2002).

I have redrawn Figure 5.3 (see Figure 5.4) to include these 'new' aspects of management and risk that outsourcing can introduce. You can see how the revised shape makes inroads into the benefits likely to be accrued from such arrangements.

5.3.3 Implications for the IT Organization

For any IT manager seeking to add outsourced service delivery to his stable, the challenges that come with the territory seem plain enough. They will revolve, as we have said, with notions of management and risk – and to mitigate against these a degree of process too. The examples I suggested in the previous section demanded, at least in part, definition of and clarity around the processes that linked the outsourced provisioning with other elements of the IT portfolio. As we said very early on, if our new IT organization leads to a decrease in process and procedure, then where it remained it would be doubly important. The elements of process that surround any outsourcing arrangement fall into that category.

It is also clear that some of the management implications need to be tackled – and that doing so will impact the shape of the IT function. My notion of the outsourcing manager as a new and potentially discrete role is not one which has been widely adopted to date, the norm being to assume that a combination of a manager from somewhere within the IT department and perhaps a colleague from the general supplier management function may, as a pair, be able to handle the outsourced relationship effectively. Indeed, in many instances they may well be able to hand hold the relationship, but will this also include the delivery of the service? So, as with the other engagement role we have focused on (that with the customer), dedication is key to success.

If the motivation for this argument were not self-evident, consideration of the implications in terms of risk adds weight to the role. The IT manager will only be able to guard against some of the 'new' risks that outsourcing inevitably introduces by ensuring that the relationship and service is managed appropriately. Many people may balk at the idea of paying a third party to provide a managed service, and then still needing to employ someone internally to provide a management layer over the top. They might argue that this lessens the benefit to be gained from outsourcing, i.e. giving back some of the potential financial benefit to be gained. Perhaps over time this may not be warranted – but I would argue that the IT manager could only afford to take such a decision with an outsourcer who had been supplying proven services over a considerable period and who worked as if they were internal to the organization. I suggest these kinds of relationship are – and by their commercial definition, have to be – few and far between.

Lastly, there is an impact on the organization in terms of the people who are involved in overseeing outsourcing arrangements, and this includes the IT manager. Much that is required is likely to be relatively mechanistic in terms of reporting, regular dialogue, prioritizing, process checking and so forth. However, there will be an element that quite clearly goes beyond this. From the outsourcer's perspective, he will expect his primary contact within the customer organization to provide direction and leadership when he needs it. We must accept that the third party cannot have carte blanche and will, at times, require decisions to be taken. On this basis, the outsourcing manager from the parent IT function must be credible at this level. It would be a mistake to appoint someone into such a position based on superb technical understanding if their management capabilities were not up to the task. Also, this individual will, in addition to providing leadership to the outsourcer, need to be able to effectively represent the external service provider within the overall IT

155

organization. Indeed, the more one thinks about this particular person, the further removed we become from a run-of-the-mill operational manager.

Resource Management

6.1 Organizations are About People

We have spent a considerable amount of time thus far addressing some of the new issues that face IT functions in today's business environment, and have looked at how some of these challenges can only be adequately met by redrafting the shape of the IT organization. In this penultimate chapter we need to recognize perhaps the most fundamental aspect of organizational shape.

No matter how we ultimately choose to define any structure, we should never move away from the clear understanding that an organization is about people. All too often structures are put together and hierarchies drawn up with scant regard for those who will inhabit individual boxes on an organogram. Managers readily assume that because the structure is 'right' it will work, and are surprised when it actually fails. For some, failure will be seen as a problem inherent in the way responsibilities and line management have been defined, and then they will move into a potentially never-ending cycle of structural adjustment. Ultimately this does two things: firstly, it destabilizes the overall function and reduces efficiency and effectiveness; and secondly, it fails to recognize that the problem may not lie in the organization per se, but in the allocation of roles to people.

With that in mind, this chapter aims to consider organizational shape from a people perspective. I will look at:

- key people criteria and how organizations can affect individuals
- general resource issues, such as fitting square pegs in square holes and how this might be done
- suggestions in terms of the HR management of IT staff

- how rewards and benefits can be used to help achieve the overall goals of the function

I also want to consider the roles we give to people and how these may align with responsibility and accountability – and how it is all too easy to think one has established effective delegation when this is not the case at all. Finally, we will consider issues around skills and knowledge management.

Throughout all this analysis I will echo some of the topics and examples already discussed in order to put the notions presented into some kind of context. Also I will again touch on management and leadership more than once. That there is a difference, I think we have already seen; that it is critical will hopefully fall out. Indeed, for some commentators such as Pearson (1992), these are not characteristics or responsibilities that should be invested in a limited number of individuals. In order to preside over a successful enterprise, Pearson suggests "involving [people] in the leadership of the organization" (Pearson, 1992).

6.2 Key People Criteria

In attempting to define some key criteria that we should consider when shaping our IT function (both from a structural perspective and then in terms of placing individuals into that structure), we need to recognize what people need, want and aspire to on two levels. The first of these relates to people as people – i.e. their instinctive needs as human beings – and the second to people as elements within an organizational whole. It would be easy to dismiss the former as irrelevant to our discussion, but I would argue that an awareness of what makes people 'tick' has to be of some value.

The obvious reference point for any generic consideration is the 'hierarchy of needs' defined by Abraham Maslow (1908–1970). Maslow categorized man's needs into five levels:

- Physiological – effectively biological needs for food, oxygen, water and warmth. These are man's primary requirements that must be satisfied.

- Safety – these needs (which follow as next in importance from physiological) relate to feeling secure in our environment; this in the sense of social structure and fabric, e.g. influenced by persecution, war, riot, violence.

- Love, affection and belonging – those feelings which aim to keep us from being lonely and alienated.

- Esteem – the need for us to respect ourselves and to gain the respect of others; a sense of confidence, value and worth.

- Self-actualization – the 'highest' level of need is about expression of the individuality of who we are based on what we do: most usually articulated as a writer's need to write, or a painter's need to paint – and the subsequent sense of restlessness if they are prevented from doing so.

Where does this come in from the perspective of an IT organization? Quite simply, the further one can support, encourage and meet the needs of an individual through Maslow's hierarchy, the more fulfilled that person will be. The IT manager can do little about the world's oxygen supply or the threat of war, but can influence senses of belonging and esteem, and potentially contribute – in a working world – to self-actualization. If 'a programmer has to program', then a manager who puts such individuals in analytical or testing roles may be doing so to the detriment of that person's 'need', thereby impacting on their happiness, contribution, efficiency and so forth. To be successful here a manager needs to understand the people who work for him, and this implies appropriate levels of communication, dialogue and feedback. Whether this is done directly or not, formally or informally, one should always be able to answer the question 'What about Dave?' with more than just 'He is a project manager'.

That these kinds of notions have already been adopted into organizational theory to a degree can be seen in comments such as this one from Pearson (1992): "motivation is based on a person's expectations". The more one is able to demonstrate the potential to meet an individual's needs – from the perspective of professional ambition – the greater likelihood of their being motivated to do well. Thus, if Tim has ambitions to become operations manager – and has shown sufficient potential to do so – then mapping out a possible route to achieve that goal (his 'self-actualization') can only benefit both the employee and the manager.

Ambition, in one flavour or another, is not the only thing that people will share – even if that ambition is not work-related. We are all managers. There will be things, some perhaps unique to us as individuals, that we manage on a day-to-day basis: our bank accounts perhaps, decisions on working hours based around train or bus timetables, or something in relation to a hobby away from work. These individual and personal management tasks will fall into one of Henry Mintzberg's types as discussed in Chapter 2; indeed, there is no reason why they should not. My point here is to disabuse ourselves of the notion that says 'I am a manager; he is not'. This is divisive. We are all managers in one way or another; some people have a greater desire or capacity for it, and a drive to realize it professionally (self-actualization, again). Managers should not feel as if they are special or superior.

This is important when one considers individuals within the context of the organizational whole. Peter F. Drucker talks about the need for high-quality personnel management based on objective setting and results (see Boylan, 2001), but there is more to being successful here than just setting out goals. We need to set appropriate targets for appropriate people. If people are not motivated or making a positive contribution then one possibility is that we, as managers, are not doing our job – it is not necessarily the case that the individual is failing. If we are going to build a successful organization we need to address the needs of individuals not only in the basic (Maslow) sense, but in the way that we manage: demonstrate "high corporate integrity" (Pearson, 1992), communicate, seek feedback, be honest, challenge positively, manage and lead – don't just manage.

6.3 Key Organizational Aspects that Affect People

Quite obviously the way an organization is structured and operates has the potential to have a major impact – both positive and negative – on those that work within it. Even assuming that we have identified and responded 'correctly' to the 'programmer who must program' and Tim's desire to, one day, become operations manager, we still have plenty of opportunity to establish a structure that will prove detrimental to all.

As I have said already, the culture of the corporate whole may be such that there is little we can do to affect this in the subset that is the IT department. In such circumstances perhaps the IT manager should be seen to acknowledge this culture in such a way so that those who work with him recognize that, whilst supporting the business as a whole, he can see other ways of achieving the same goals. One should never underestimate the positive power that can be invested in an individual when overcoming a generally negative situation – and, unfortunately, the negative power when deflating something that is intrinsically positive. Remaining open and honest – even in a culture that supports political double-dealing and agenda setting – can work wonders. As Pearson (1992) suggests, "explicit openness will inhibit dishonesty at all levels and also serve to ensure consistency of integrity so that trust can be built up with all stakeholders"; such trust – and the associated respect it will inevitably bring – can be vital.

So what should we look out for organizationally in terms of those things which can impact people as people?

- Following on from Maslow, Eisenstat et al. (2001) suggest that matching resources with opportunities presents an organizational issue. This from two points of view: firstly in finding the programming job for the programmer, and secondly in attempting to ensure that when fresh opportunities do appear they are not always given to the same people. The latter is a tricky issue because the tendency will be to give such opportunities to those that will grasp and make the most of them – which will, of course, usually be the same people over and over again. The role of the resource pool may help here in the sense that if the opportunity is offered to the 'pool', more people may (in theory at least) have access to it.

- Line management structure – and line managers – can also impact the effectiveness of people. By this I do not mean the structure – hierarchical, flat or otherwise – but the way in which line management is executed and the potential conflicts within relationships. There is probably little we can do about personality conflicts except keep an eye open for them and try to remove them (perhaps through reallocation of roles, etc.) before they get out of hand. In terms of line management style, the trick must be to ensure consistency of approach – which helps to defuse protestations of bias – and to follow the same method yourself. Of course if this leads to absolute collapse, then it probably says something about your own management style!

- Associated with line management structure, I would argue that there can be a negative impact if individuals a) are too far removed from the top tier of management within the organization and/or b) never get to see their own manager because they have too many direct reports. For the former, encourage an 'open door' policy and get your managers to 'walk the floor' occasionally – as you must too. For the latter, HR guidelines suggest seven to ten direct reports is the right kind of balance for any line manager; not a bad target to aim for.

● Bureaucracy within an organization will seldom have a positive impact on the people upon whom it is inflicted. We have talked about the need for process and controls often enough, and there will need to be associated paperwork to support this; but burdening people with over-officiousness can never have a positive outcome. If people can complete a reasonably detailed weekly timesheet in five minutes which will give managers enough information to know if their projects are on track, then why invent a procedure that takes twenty minutes longer just to get that last 5% of detail? At this kind of level people will make it up anyway – after all, they already do so for the five-minute exercise! The key here is about being pragmatic and, to a degree, ruthless. If there is no real need for any item of bureaucracy, then bin it. If there is, then articulate it; individuals will be happier to comply if they understand and can see why it is needed.

Obviously there will be more. The important thing here is to recognize that getting an organization working well is not just about having the most perfect layout on your organogram; how the structure is implemented will be of equal importance in the long run.

6.4 Resource Issues

6.4.1 What Kind of Person am I?

Knowing what makes a person tick is about more than good communication and understanding desires or ambitions. Knowing that someone wants only to program or that they are aiming at senior management can help prevent inappropriate moves and encourage appropriate ones. However, leaving Maslow aside, this is only half of the equation from an individual's perspective. Ambition and self-actualization is about 'what' people do, not how they do it. That this second half of the formula is critical has already been suggested in our earlier discussions around management styles – Zeus, Apollo, etc. – and through notions that an inappropriate management approach can turn a perfectly adequate structure into something that appears fatally flawed. If we are going to give ourselves the best possible chance of creating a successful organization then we must try and put people into jobs that suit them – as well as into roles that they wish to perform.

In the same way that we chose Maslow for an illustration of the needs hierarchy, there is perhaps a default analysis here that we can follow. Meredith Belbin (born 1926) devised a form of personality profiling which, in breaking individuals down into nine primary 'team role' types, offers an objective mechanism for fitting people to roles by dint of their personal characteristics. The fact that these are 'team' roles is critical, i.e. how individuals perform within situations of team dynamics is obviously fundamental to the shaping of any organizational structure. Belbin's groupings are as follows:

- Co-ordinator: someone who organizes the efforts of a group of individuals

- Shaper: a person who seeks to influence outcomes, direction and patterns; likes to overcome obstacles

- Plant: a creative, problem-solving person; good with new ideas and strategies

- Monitor evaluator: someone who likes to undertake thorough analysis; an accurate judge who can arbitrate between options

- Resource investigator: an out-going, people-focused engagement person; good communicator and networker

- Team worker: supportive to a larger group, making positive contributions to team spirit; diplomatic

- Implementer: a practical person who executes against defined plans; systematic

- Completer–finisher: someone who dislikes mistakes and inaccuracies; detail-conscious

- Specialist: a person who can input particular threads of knowledge and expertise into a group; can translate 'general' into 'technical'

How might this prove useful to us? Table 6.1 considers each of Belbin's characteristics against a number of IT-related jobs to suggest how well suited – or not – they might be to each.

In the list in Table 6.1 there is no category that explicitly states 'Manager'. However, those who have achieved managerial status will also major in

Table 6.1. Belbin's Team Roles and IT Jobs

	Co-ordinator	Shaper	Plant	Monitor evaluator	Resource investigator	Team worker	Implementer	Completer–finisher	Specialist
Project Manager	✓		✗			✓		✓	
Business Analyst	✗			✓		✓			
Test Manager				✓				✓	✓
Database Administrator		✗	✓		✗				✓
Outsourcing Manager	✓				✓		✓	✓	
Project Planner			✗	✓	✗			✗	
Help Desk Engineer	✗	✗			✗	✓	✓		✗
Engagement Manager	✓				✓		✗		✗

Some suggestions as to 'fit': ✓ = likely positive match; ✗ = likely negative match

one of Belbin's core traits – which will quite obviously influence their style of management and the culture they create. For example, a manager who is a Monitor Evaluator is likely to operate a function that is ordered, well-structured and reasonably thorough; on the other hand, the Resource Investigator may operate at the other extreme, with loose processes and controls, and a culture based on personality. For an IT manager making senior appointments within his organization, understanding preferred team roles for the individuals concerned could be very useful.

Belbin goes some way along this path through the identification of two types of leader: the solo leader and the team leader. The former acts more as a dictator (one of Handy's Zeus-types) and would be poorly suited to an entrepreneurial post; the latter, a mission-driven delegator and diversifier, would struggle in a situation where a very strong and power-centric management style was needed. As with Handy, Mintzberg and McGregor, Belbin's analysis contributes to an overlapping panoply of study that can provide – together or individually – important indicators for the resource manager.

6.4.2 What Kind of Person is Needed?

In some respects an IT manager finds himself coming at his organization structure from at least three perspectives. The first – and primary force – is the influence placed upon it by the needs and demands of the business; he needs to establish a function that is capable of delivering against commercial drivers. Secondly, he will be influenced by what already exists. In very few circumstances will an IT manager have a true 'green field' opportunity where he faces no constraints whatsoever. If an IT manager approaches the task of structure definition with a strategy and ideal organization firmly in his mind, these will almost inevitably need to be seen as medium- to long-term goals as he must initially support that which is already in place. Thus, if his plan is to outsource the help desk function currently manned by in-house personnel, the timing of the move – and the organizational shift that accompanies it – will be determined by the process he needs to go through to find and then engage a suitable partner. The need to support legacy application systems or technologies is perhaps the most significant compromiser of organizational plans.

The third perspective placed upon the structure is the people perspective we are discussing now. It might be possible for the IT manager to find ideal roles and responsibilities for all his staff within his ideal structure – however, he will be very lucky if this is not compromised by the previous two fields of influence. Indeed, the personnel consideration sits at the very bottom of the organizational shape food chain.

This is illustrated in Figure 6.1, where people considerations sit below both business and technological drivers – yet it is also represented as the base of the triangle, or the bedrock upon which success will be built. Getting the right people will enable the technology, and enabling the technology will drive business benefit. Thus, making no effort at getting the best people–role fit is not really an option, and therefore the question 'what kind of person is needed?' should still be asked.

The kind of table shown (Table 6.1) could be used to assist in answering this question if one had sufficient details on individuals in terms of formal Belbin analysis. Of course, it does not have to be Belbin that is used as the analytical tool. 'DISC' profiling – which identifies people's traits in the areas of Dominance, Influence, Stability and Conscientiousness – is another, simpler tool which could also generate a matrix similar to that shown above. Such profiling methods are not in general use, however, and tend to be driven at a corporate level; thus it is more than likely that

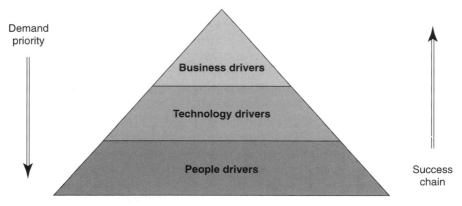

Figure 6.1. Organizational Influencers

the IT manager will have nothing to aid him in this regard (although instigating something locally should always be an option). Even the absence of anything formal need not stop effort being placed in this area. After all, you will know the kinds of skills needed, and you should know something about your people. For example, if, as Foote et al. (2001) suggest, customer-facing units "are amorphous" and need "a broad range of talent", it is highly likely that the IT manager will be able to identify those within his organization who fall into this category. In fact, the whole process is much less daunting than it might appear. After all, the demands placed upon him by the technology will distil certain skill-sets – for example, a Microsoft Office specialist could not work as an Oracle Database Administrator without extensive training – and it may be that the IT manager will be left to make resourcing decisions around leadership and engagement areas. Here being able to answer the question 'what kind of person is needed?' – and, hopefully, being able to find a decent fit – will go a long way towards providing a sound basis for future success.

6.4.3 Recognizing the Organizational Imperative

I would even go so far as to suggest that tackling issues around resource 'fit' are absolutely imperative for the success of any IT organization. We can illustrate the implications of taking no action in this area through a simple theoretical example. I have taken the illustration (Figure 6.1) and added a further base layer to the model, giving Figure 6.2; this layer represents the organizational structure which ultimately supports all three sets of drivers above it. On the assumption that nothing is perfect, I am

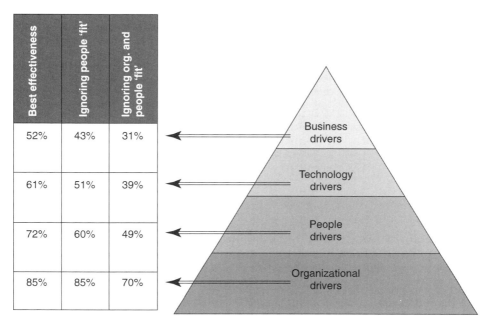

Best effectiveness	Ignoring people 'fit'	Ignoring org. and people 'fit'
52%	43%	31%
61%	51%	39%
72%	60%	49%
85%	85%	70%

Figure 6.2. *Organizational Pyramid*

going to assume that an IT manager will achieve a success rate of some-where around 85% in terms of effectiveness at each level. This implies that his organization will run at around 15% lower than maximum efficiency simply because it is highly unlikely that it will ever be perfect or fluid enough to meet shifting day-to-day demands. Similarly, despite all efforts at addressing the resource fit conundrum via Belbin, DISC or whatever, the IT manager achieves around an 85% match in terms of people to jobs. Utilization of technology – again never perfect – sits at the same mark, as will an ability to deliver against critical business drivers (many of which may be unknown or unarticulated). Assuming these performances are compound, we can see that ultimately he will satisfy 52% of all potential business drivers.

If we now assume that the IT manager chooses not to take into consideration resource drivers and pays no real attention in terms of who sits where in his structure, see what happens to the overall effectiveness if we cut the 85% at this level down to 70%. His headline effectiveness falls to 43% – and if he fails to start with a properly considered organizational structure (another fall to 70%), this drops even further to 31%. Obviously these numbers are purely hypothetical and would undoubtedly be difficult to measure and prove, however the logic is perfectly clear and undeniable.

Protestations that there is never enough time to undertake an in-depth resource analysis with a view to tackling the 'fit' issues under discussion here will, in many cases, have some degree of validity. Indeed, it may be prohibitively expensive to send every member of the IT function for an assessment. On these objections I would make two observations. Firstly, the vast majority of companies have in place some form of annual performance appraisal process – which, I suspect, is rarely followed to the letter. These review methodologies may already have (or after slight amendment may be open to have) much of the necessary information about not only what a person does or has done, but also how they go about it. My second point would be to suggest that as an initial priority there is no need to send all and sundry for assessment; after all, a large proportion of the IT resource pool will be technically biased to such a degree that what you need them to do will be relatively clear cut. Where deepening understanding may be of most value is with those individuals who are likely to be offered man-management or engagement roles – areas where installing the wrong person or wrong type of person can have very serious consequences. So start there.

But even undertaking such assessments must not be seen in an end in itself. How many enterprises do make the investment, but then do nothing with the information they have gathered? Someone may return from a Belbin assessment certain in the knowledge that they are a wall-to-wall shaper, only to discover that their role – which demands a Completer–Finisher and in which they have been unhappy for months – does not change. The only thing that will have been achieved is that the individual now knows why they have been unsettled. Even though we are working within a technical function, we must recognize that in some roles the personality mix is far more important than the systems skill-set. Given that the background for the majority in this realm (including the IT manager) is likely to be highly technical, arriving at such clarity of thought can take years – if it ever comes at all.

6.4.4 Fitting the Right People In

Theorists and writers such as Elton Mayo (1880–1949) have suggested that for many people maximizing the performance of an individual in an organization can be stimulated more by personal satisfaction than economic gain. The assumption that simply paying an employee an extra 10% on their existing salary will ensure continuing – or improved – effectiveness has, to a certain degree, lost its credibility. If job perform-ance equates directly with role satisfaction, then the position and responsibility one has within the organization is obviously paramount.

The critical aspects of this 'functional fit' extend even further. Mayo sug-gested that a sense of belonging was important too, i.e. not only how one's role was a match for both personal and technical abilities and ambitions, but also how an individual worked within a group. For exam-ple, if there is a senior IT management team which is made up of five Zeus-type managers and one Dionysian 'shaper', then we can be reason-ably confident that there will be times when the latter feels uncomfort-able in his peer group. If this disquiet translates to a lack of satisfaction, then performance – assuming the logic holds – would fall. Such a situa-tion is not uncommon, of course. Many managers will – subconsciously or not – try to ensure their direct reports are like-minded people, often without sufficient regard to the roles that these people must fill. The out-come of such a move is to potentially enjoy a closely-knit peer group, but one where an individual may struggle to execute their responsibilities in a satisfactory manner.

Under such circumstances – and particularly where there are instances such as a single rogue character amongst like-profiled managers – a sec-ond, informal level of group peering can begin to emerge. Here, the dis-affected shaper (or whatever) may begin to bond with other shapers in the organization; perhaps others who are unhappy with the overall ethos of the management team, their direct line manager, and so on. If this happens, these informal groups can gain significant influence, which could be very negative if the impact was a destabilizing one. Such circumstances can lead to 'political' in-fighting between factions of the same 'team' based upon different views as to how things should be. In organizations where the overall corporate culture is well known and accepted this is less likely to happen; but where the business – or, more particularly, the IT function – does not have any defined culture, there must be some vulnerability to political instability, particularly in embry-onic or new-born organizations.

These considerations do re-emphasize the need for the IT manager to try and get the right person in the right job. Yet this is obviously a com-plex undertaking in some instances, particularly in the modern IT func-tion where new resource models are needed, and where new types of skill – for example engagement expertise – is critical. There can be no easy answer. Analyses may unfortunately offer conflicting answers as to which people should fill which jobs, and it would seem inevitable that compromise may be required along the way. It is partly because of these outcomes that I believe we can assume we will never achieve 100% effectiveness from either our organization or our people.

At the management layer, fitting in the right kind of manager will offer the potential for the most significant successes and failures. This is not to belittle any non-management role, but rather recognition of the influence such people can have over the rest of the workforce. Max Weber (1864–1920), in his 1924 volume *Theory of Social and Economic Organization* (see Boylan, 2001), talked about the different kinds of management authority that exist within an organization:

- Rational – an authority based on the maximization of performance via a system of rules and procedures

- Traditional – the authority invested in someone by right of their office or position held within the hierarchy

- Charismatic – bestowed authority which other individuals are happy to voluntarily invest in a manager on the basis of their personal qualities (this, in my mind, is a definition of real leadership)

Given an IT function with a broad remit, one can argue that a mix of these types of manager may well benefit the overall enterprise: the IT manager or head of engagement may need to be charismatic; the leader of the project management pool, rational; the operations manager, traditional. We can also see how some of the analysis we have already referred to – Zeus/Apollo, Completer–Finisher/Shaper and so forth – may help us in our assessment of both roles and people, and then the accurate alignment of the two. One prerequisite here is likely to be the need for a 'clearly defined sphere of competence' or scope of role.

6.4.5 HR in the IT Organization

Given that the 'people' aspects of IT organizations are becoming increasingly influential over the relative success of the entire function, it is unfortunate if this is not recognized in terms of the relationship between IT and HR departments. In traditional personnel models, the department acts more or less as a generic support function. In addition to managing things like payroll, disciplinary processes and recruitment, HR most often is responsible for the procedures around the annual performance review cycle and associated spin-offs, such as development and training.

In many models, the HR department may – like other general service functions – offer a prime or named contact for the IT department, with the aim of ensuring that there is a single conduit for IT personnel issues, and that there is one person within HR who maintains a reasonable degree of familiarity with the systems teams. This has been acceptable in the past, but I would argue that – given the new kind of IT organizational model we are seeking – a number of flaws in this structure are now being exposed:

- The HR representative does not know enough members of the IT function. Their contact will be primarily through the top team and a small number of other key man managers. They will not be in a position to make a telling contribution in any debates about individuals, personalities and roles.

- The IT function needs engagement with HR at a deeper and more 'personalized' level than simply through a central agency whose job is to act as a conduit for corporate policy. For example, if the annual appraisal process that exists does have the potential for offering the IT function additional meaningful benefit, then there should be a way to engage in a dialogue that allows for local enhancement and modification – all of this to be managed by an HR professional.

- Too often all HR-related responsibilities are delegated to individual line managers within an IT organization, often resulting in a wide discrepancy in terms of the quality of staff-related engagement – sometimes to the extreme of whether or not appraisals are actually carried out. People who work in IT are not HR professionals, and whilst it is obviously incumbent on them to execute all appropriate man-management duties, such requests represent the extreme to which many can actually venture.

My argument to address these issues and tackle the challenge of getting solid, reliable, meaningful and adopted HR policies and procedures within the IT organization is to have a personnel professional resident full-time within the IT organization (assuming this is warranted by size of function of course). This individual – needing to have a 'dotted line' report into the central HR function – would report to the IT manager and would be responsible for:

- Ensuring any performance appraisal process was followed, including ensuring the scheduling and execution of annual and interim meetings between staff and their line managers.

- Collation and retention of all documentation in relation to that process; once again this would give a quality assurance (QA) element to the role.

- Maintenance of all training and development plans in accordance with both the appraisal process and any one-off project demands.

- Acting as a specialist resource to co-ordinate, arrange or administer any analytical assessment (e.g. Belbin) in accordance with the needs of the IT function.

- Ensure the currency of all role definitions and job descriptions, again in a QA capacity.

- Provide an arbitration service and co-ordination point in the event of any local disputes, and for any 'salary levelling' process which may need to take place at annual review time.

- Understand the general IT resource market, salary conditions, trends, etc.

- Act as a consultant to the IT manager (and other senior managers) around organizational issues such as structural shape, reporting lines, personnel 'fit' and so on.

The advantages to the IT manager of adopting such an approach will be to ensure that there is a consistent – and consistently applied – set of HR processes which can be seen to be impartial and can be followed even-handedly across the organization. Not only that, having such an unbiased organizational insight available locally – invested in someone who, through day-to-day contact, knows the staff well – can provide the IT manager with valuable additional input when it comes to tackling issues such as resource fit and team dynamics.

6.4.6 Rewards and Benefits

Before leaving resource issues, I would like to touch on the subject of reward and recognition. In the previous section we identified that simply paying people more money was no guarantee of any particular level of performance, this being superseded in many cases by job satisfaction as the primary motivator. However, we must still acknowledge that pay is an important – and highly emotive – consideration for us all as individuals.

Adopting the suggestion with respect to having an HR person within the IT organization itself can assist greatly here. It is not uncommon for people (in whichever function they work) to become unsettled or demotivated by feeling that there are those in the business who have been given pay awards that were not merited. How many of us have not come across the situation where one particular line manager is either more generous with their pay reviews than another, or can simply argue their case better than anyone else? The independent HR professional, there to oversee and QA the entire process, should help to reduce the kinds of disquiet caused by these sorts of event.

Indeed, they can offer the IT manager a much greater service than simply acting as policeman and arbiter. Traditionally, individuals have been rewarded at the end of the annual cycle dependent on a number of essentially subjective categories: how well they have done; how important they are felt to be to the business; and how much money is available in the pay 'pot'. Our new organizational structure challenges this simple and argumentative process in a number of ways. Firstly, given that the IT manager should be addressing the performance and improvement of his entire function, there are likely to be more metrics available to assess exactly what has been delivered. Secondly, given that we are also moving towards a structure that contains a greater mix of skills, we should recognize that simple technical measures may not apply to some people – an engagement manager or the HR person, for example. And thirdly, with an increasing trend towards providing 'optional' bonus payments in addition to base salaries, the IT manager finds himself with a more complex – but also more flexible – way of rewarding his staff. Sales people are, quite naturally, rewarded based on tangible orders won; for Eisenstat et al. (2001), the key for opportunity-based resources – such as the engagement manager's – will be getting reward and recognition right.

How should we tackle this then? I would advocate a four-tier model as follows:

● Base component. This might be a 'flat rate' increase in basic salary that is dependent upon both the performance of the company and the performance of the IT function as a whole. I would suggest that this should account for somewhere in the region of 25% of the available annual uplift pot.

- Team target component. Short-term bonus-targeted activities should have two elements; the first of these is individual-specific, the second is team-related. This component, earned at the team level, should again equate to 25% of the whole.

- Individual target component. The other half of the item above, again at 25% of the available pot.

- Personal bonus component (annual). The final quarter of the monies available is awarded based on achievement of specific measures in relation to roles and responsibilities; for example, hitting an SLA within operations, or delivering projects to time and budget. These, as with the previous two items, are entirely measurable and should be open to calculation, i.e. achieving 75% of the targets set gains 75% of the potential bonus available (or however this is calculated).

How should the short-term bonus-targeted activities work? The personal bonus component relates to individual targets that are set at the beginning of the year and reviewed at its conclusion (although these may be added to over time, of course). Thus the operations manager may have a target to ensure an SLA of 99.5% for the e-mail system is achieved over a twelve-month period – something that can be cascaded down through the organization, of course. The target components are, I suggest, short-term specifics that are set and reviewed quarterly. They relate to tactical deliverables that are relevant over the coming period and remain active for only that period. A developer may, perhaps, get a specific target to make modifications to an ERP module within a defined time-window. If they do so, they earn something towards their bonus; if not, then the opportunity is lost. Such specific and immediate goals can help keep momentum and delivery constant throughout the year. Additionally, these targets will be 'split' in the sense that for each one hit, credit goes to both the individual and the team within which the work is carried out. Such a mechanism can foster positive collaborative working relationships.

I will conclude here with a simple example of this kind of process in action. In Table 6.2 we have an IT function of four people. The total pot available to the IT manager at the end of the year is $16,000. This gives him $4,000 to apportion across each of the reward components. The table shows a) the percentage of individual or team targets hit, b) how this translates into a relative percentage across the four resources, and c) the financial equivalent.

Table 6.2. Pay and Bonus Awards

	Alan			Brian			Charles			David		
	% hit	% equiv.	$ (,000s)	% hit	% equiv.	$ (,000s)	% hit	% equiv.	$ (,000s)	% hit	% equiv.	$ (,000s)
Base component	-	25	1.0	-	25	1.0	-	25	1.0	-	25	1.0
Team component	50	25	1.0	80	40	1.6	20	10	0.4	50	25	1.0
Individual component	60	30	1.2	20	10	0.4	60	30	1.2	60	30	1.2
Bonus component	70	28	1.1	40	16	0.6	90	36	1.5	50	20	0.8
Total award	$4,300			$3,600			$4,100			$4,000		

We can see from this how the system has benefited or penalized each of our members of staff. Brian, for example, although he may be a team player (as evidenced by the percentage of team goals to which he has contributed), has consistently failed to deliver against his personal objectives and receives a below-average award. Charles, on the other hand, has contributed less to 'team' goals but is a high performer from an individual perspective. The largest award goes to Alan, who has demonstrated a balance of team and personal delivery across the year. This may seem over-complex, but it does have significant benefits in terms of improving delivery and working within a fair and equitable reward structure: the weightings and ratios can be adjusted to suit particular business models, cultures and circumstances; and the targets themselves can be made role-dependent, therefore helping to address the issues around appropriate rewards for 'non-technical' staff. It is also, of course, another argument for having an HR person sitting within the function!

6.5 'What Does He Do?'

6.5.1 The Bottom Line

Once an organization has been established and is perceived to be functioning well, there is a danger of complacency setting in. Obviously if appropriate measures, targets and rewards have been set, then a reasonably constant monitoring and reporting on performance will help to ensure that too much focus is not lost. However, 'blind spots' can materialize within any structure in terms of individuals' contributions. Let us assume I am an IT manager who has a structure in place that has been performing well for over a year, with consistent achievement of targets and an improving trend across all segments of the department. Additionally I have a management team of six who have helped me steer us to our present position. I am comfortable with this team and, as long as we continue to improve, then why should I consider changing it?

Well, it could be that part of the function has improved and gelled so well that the head of that subset – and a member of my management team – has become increasingly less and less involved with the day-to-day operation of that for which he is responsible. It is running so well that he is now really occupied only about 40% of the time. Given that changes might upset the status quo, this is something that he has chosen not to point out to me. When it does come to my attention, what should I do? It would be all too easy to either agree to ignore the situation for the present, or to manufacture some 'additional' duties to fill the gap. If the latter were needed and constructive all well and good, but if not …?

Often in spite of their own style, approach and leanings, there may well be times when managers need to head for the bottom line and ask the question 'what does he do?' Given the kind of drivers faced by the IT function, the days when passengers could be carried should be long gone; and with IT managers themselves quite rightly being measured on the performance of their function, then anyone who is not fully contributing – either as a direct result of their own performance or, as in the case above, because of an inadequate or misaligned role – is having a negative impact on the effectiveness of the function. There are two key questions which I suggest should be asked of each individual from time to time, either directly by their line manager or privately by themselves: 'what have I done to improve the business?' and 'would you miss me?' I will return to these momentarily.

For the IT manager there is an additional 'bottom line' for the organization he presides over. At the end of the twentieth century much play was made of corporate or functional 'mission statements'. These were intended as a 'call to arms' for the troops within those functions; a kind of rallying cry behind which everyone could line up. More often than not, mission statements became vacuous meaningless phrases to which people paid little heed; more effort was spent in defining them than was ever recouped through their being followed.

Whilst not a personal fan of mission statements, they can act as a simple QA for the IT manager. Can he, for instance, articulate a mission statement for his entire organization? Is it possible to define, in a single sentence, what each subset or element of the department is there to achieve? If so, is there one single metric that can be taken from each mission statement and added to the organizational reporting whole? If so, then not only will there exist a series of 'fluffy' objectives which have a hard centre and behind which people can pull, there will also be a means of measuring them. If, on the other hand, a mission for a subset of the organization cannot be articulated, then I suggest that this may cast a doubt over whether or not it should exist. For example, an IT manager – knowing that he needs to keep a firm grasp of his overall strategy – chooses to appoint a small group with a 'strategic' remit. After some deliberation, he finds that he can neither articulate their mission, nor define metrics for them. This does not mean that he does not need a strategy of course; but what it might imply is that there might be other organizational ways in which his goals can be achieved.

6.5.2 'What Have I Done to Improve the Business?'; 'Would You Miss Me?'

Being open and honest about one's own performance or position in an organization will be difficult for most people. How many would not answer 'yes' if prompted with the question about the organization missing their input? However, in pursuing the 'bottom line' from a resource and structure perspective, we need a mechanism to not only ensure that we have answers to these two key questions, but that they are actually asked in the first place.

In one company where I worked, I kept a single sheet of A4 pinned above my desk with the words 'What have I done to improve the business today?' writ large. It acted as a kind of mantra, and – based on its location – it was one I could not miss seeing every day. If I left work having not had a particularly good day, the notice stabbed me gently; if there had been some successes during the day, it acted as a positive reinforcer. It was good being able to answer in the affirmative. I am not advocating this kind of prompt for every employee within an IT function, but we need to ensure that the question is at least 'visible'.

Of course any performance appraisal process – either annual, or driven by monthly or quarterly targets – will provide a mechanism to identify tangible deliverables. These are all well and good, but their formality takes away a degree of the personal spontaneity of knowing one has made a difference – and that is really what it is all about. Having said at the outset that IT functions were there for the managed delivery of technology-driven change, people working within the function should be able to point to things that they have worked on and say 'Because I did A, B or C, X, Y or Z will have improved within the business'. What A, B or C might actually be will obviously vary from person to person; to a certain extent it does not matter what it is – or if it is formally recognized within the performance or bonus appraisal system. The immediate benefit is largely one around the bolstering of a feeling of self-worth and contribution, which can only remind us of Maslow.

A suggestion for trying to instil this kind of culture might be to instigate a simple round-table element at each team meeting where, one by one, people are asked to nominate something that they have done in the previous week which would provide a positive answer to the question 'What have I done to improve the business?' Ultimately of course, the IT manager needs to be able to answer that same question in the affirmative for every member of his entire team.

Asking the 'Would you miss me?' question is obviously not something for an open forum. Indeed, even in private it is a much harder question to be truly honest about. For most people one would assume – or hope! – that the answer would be 'yes'; but this will actually depend on whether or not it were approached from the perspective of missing the person as an individual or missing having someone performing that function. If the former, then the 'yes' should still stand; if the latter, then in most cases the answer will be 'no' because someone else could be brought in to carry out the duties concerned.

This is a valid question for the IT manager, of course; indeed, for the person at the top of the organizational tree the wording would be subtly different, i.e. 'Would I miss them?' This could be asked at any point in time. In the case of our manager working at only 40% capacity, how this question was answered might lead to radically different outcomes. If the response was 'no' because his direct reports were capable of running the subfunction and taking on any residual management tasks, then the manager might be moved out. If the answer was 'yes' because he was the IT manager's 'right-hand man', then additional duties and responsibilities would inevitably be found.

This is a less easy question to get people to ask themselves – particularly as it has potentially negative and destabilizing consequences – but it is important. People should be encouraged to ensure that the only possible answer is 'yes'. How might they do this? Engagement managers might build up such a solid and intimate relationship with their business partners that they simply could not be moved out without damaging the relationship. Outsourcing managers could follow the same tack, giving the IT manager unparalleled insights and interfaces into the outsourcer's organization. Project managers could, time after time, deliver projects in such a reliable and consistent fashion that they become the 'point men' on all major undertakings. Getting people to think about not just what or how they do their job, but also to get that extra element of quality into it – going the extra yard – can make all the difference, not only to them as people, but to the function as a whole.

6.5.3 Is This About the Person or Their 'Slot' in the Organization?

When there is a negative outcome to these kinds of deliberations – perhaps the IT manager decides that someone has contributed nothing towards improving the business and that this particular person would not be missed – there is a need for final clarification of what this actually means before any action is taken. We cannot escape the fact that, with people not being identical, there will be some negative threads as far as relationships are concerned within the organization. However much we try to ensure that these do not interfere with making correct logical decisions, they still undoubtedly will. Thus, simply deciding that an individual is surplus to requirements should not be the final word on the subject.

Having our HR person within the function can help under these circumstances. For example, if this conclusion has been arrived at as a result of due process then there would be someone who can confirm that the observation is not only a fair one but also based on solid ground. Even so, the key issue may still not have been tackled. I suggest that for any person who is perceived as a 'non-performer' (however that might be defined) two possibilities exist: firstly, that they are simply that; and secondly, it is an underlying problem with the role they have which needs to be tackled.

In the first instance – where the problem really is a personnel issue – there should be a considerable amount of credible evidence to support the conclusion that this individual is somehow not up to scratch:

- They may be woefully short in terms of technical ability – but such a conclusion can only be drawn if they have been given the opportunity to learn the appropriate skills.

- They may have an aptitude problem – the skills are there, but they have problems in applying or motivating themselves which may, in turn, lead to a lack of reliability, lateness and so on.

- The problem may be one of personality – they are particularly unpleasant, rude, chauvinistic, racist or whatever, i.e. something within their make-up that leads them to be generally disliked and failing to fit within the overall organization.

Of these three, the latter is one that can lead to the assumption that the first two also apply, i.e. because we do not like them, we assume in them lack of ability and aptitude. Again having an HR person on hand all the time can help to mitigate against these kinds of conclusions being drawn – and protect against their sometimes unfortunate consequences.

Our second possibility is one relating not to the person, but to the role they have been given. Here again there are a couple of critical questions to ask:

- Is it the role itself that is invalid, i.e. no matter who was given the responsibility concerned, would it be impossible to make a success of it? Under these circumstances we are talking about there being a weakness in the formal organizational structure, and thus there could be a need for some kind of review.

- If the role is valid, then the issue may well be the 'fit' of the individual. Everyone likes the person concerned and respects their abilities, so it is difficult to understand how they are failing to deliver. It could be a situation where we have put a 'Plant' in a role that needs a 'Resource Evaluator' in order to ensure success. Here we could again look to a review of the organization, only this time not from a structural perspective, but one of role allocation.

The message here is simple enough; if there are obvious problems with people performing so as to fail to contribute to the overall goals of the function, then we need to ensure that the issue really is with the person and not a logical outcome of organizational weakness.

6.6 Roles, Responsibilities and Accountability

6.6.1 What Jobs Do and What They Deliver

In our previous section we have suggested at least two reasons for having a clear understanding about roles; the first was around building mission statements – what a role or collection of roles 'do' – and the second related to judging the performance of an individual in less than ideal circumstances – what a role or collection of roles should 'deliver'. These build on other notions that suggest the criticality of defining particular roles: understanding what type of person is required (as with Belbin); knowing what kind of management style may be required (Handy et al.); being able to articulate, in concrete terms, the metrics associated with roles to enable reporting on performance.

As with many personnel-related themes in an IT function, often insufficient or inconsistent regard is paid to role definition and specification. Thought tends only to be given to these items when it is time to fill a vacancy, and then the procedure is most usually to find the latest document template, fill it in as quickly as possible (without regard for any interconnecting roles), and then consign the specification to a generic waste bin post-appointment. This is plainly an inadequate way of operating, and once again suggests a use for an HR specialist within the IT function.

Having a professional – but not overly bureaucratic – approach to defining what roles do and what they deliver is perhaps even more important as we move away from strictly hierarchical and technology-lead organizations into structures that are more varied and fluid. The kind of ethos propounded by Frederick Taylor of workers methodically selected, trained and aligned to specific fields of expertise is no longer the norm; indeed, his very basic premiss that "worker = work, and management = responsibility" (see Boylan, 2001) no longer holds. Even the term 'manager' – a signifier of seniority – is under some threat as it becomes more or less meaningless. An engagement manager, in looking after a business relationship, may 'manage' no other people, thus violating the original implication of the term. This kind of shift – away from traditional 'management' posts – is another reason to support appropriate role definition. Indeed, Day and Wendler's (1998) claim that "capturing the value from a relational form calls for careful planning and continuous monitoring" also implies that the roles within the relational form must, in turn, be clear enough to provide a mechanism for that monitoring.

How might we approach role definition then? What things might we need to consider?

- Deliverables: the tangible things that people will be able to read, see, touch and check that are the logical output of a person performing this function. Potentially we might also want to include any inputs or dependencies for the role. A baker's deliverable is bread, given the raw ingredients of yeast, flour, water, salt, etc. For an engagement manager, the deliverables will be around the control of programmes and projects in a particular area, and will be dependent on gaining the co-operation and input from both business and systems colleagues.

- Measurables: how those deliverables or outputs will be measured. This can be in terms of time, budget or quality, but should always be a numeric value. Our engagement manager may most likely be measured on delivery of business benefit and customer satisfaction.

- Activities: what someone is expected to do in order to achieve their deliverables: running programme boards perhaps, regular meetings with project managers, delivery of regular programme reports, and so forth.

- Attitude: the 'how' in terms of an expectation for doing the role. An engagement manager would be expected to be professional, polite, courteous, articulate and confident.

This list does not imply reams and reams of useless documentation. I would suggest that a few bullet points against each heading should suffice; indeed, if the description were to extend beyond a single page of A4, then we should throw it away and start again. Ultimately the definition should be good enough for a prospective employee to know what is expected of them, and how they are expected to perform; it should act as a check for any person in post to see if they are delivering in accordance with the expectations of the role; and for the IT manager, it should act as a means of justifying the role both within his organization and to anyone who should question it.

Note that nowhere in the bulleted list above have I used the term 'job'. In an ideal world, we should be talking about roles here and not jobs – and recognize that a 'post holder' may take on a number of roles.

6.6.2 Defining Boundaries

For every role within an organization certain boundaries will exist, and thus far our four broad categories make no explicit mention of these. Such boundaries relate to the degree of responsibility that must go with each role, and are usually associated with authority and decision-making. Even if one has articulated the specification well in terms of the deliverables, measurables, activities and attitude, the role holder will still want to know how far they can 'go' or are expected to 'go' in pursuit of their goals; where is that line they should not cross?

A simple example: It is not unusual for a company to have a strict tier of financial authorization based on degree of seniority within the business. Every single position must, by definition, reside somewhere on that particular ladder, and therefore have a ceiling on expenditure authority. I would suggest that in far too many cases these limits are a) not widely known, and b) never included on any job specification. The first time an individual discovers that they exist is when they are hauled over the coals for approving a purchase order that is beyond their authority. Given that this kind of boundary is a numeric one, where it can be relatively black and white as to its transgression, then surely it should be included within the role definition. 'How far can I go?'; 'You can spend up to £10,000 without needing extra approval.'

Even though this is obviously a significant step in the right direction, one problem faced here is that unwritten caveats may exist; 'You can spend up to £10,000 without needing extra approval – unless I decide, after the event, that you did in fact need to clear it with me,' This is the kind of problem organizations continually face in terms of giving individuals the responsibility to deliver something, but then taking away any authority to effect the outcome. In the kind of model I am advocating we should be clear on this point; either someone has – or does not have – the responsibility to spend a certain amount of money. If they do, then they are likely to be a budget holder either at programme, project or functional level; if they hold a budget, then appropriate reporting and controls will soon identify whether or not they are exceeding their budget. This is the important thing, and not fogging the issue of authority. As soon as people are stung by the situation where they have been told they can authorize a certain amount and are then castigated for doing so, where is their incentive to take the risk of doing so again?

This kind of concrete choice – and the 'numeric' visibility of that choice – is much easier to cater for than the second element of 'how far can I go?' This resides around the notion of decision-making. Anyone with a responsibility to deliver something will be making decisions all the time, be they the IT manager, a business analyst or a help desk engineer. Most of the time these decisions will be run-of-the-mill, obvious, and with low levels of impact if they go awry. But what about the 'bigger' decisions? It is obviously not possible to tell someone that they can make decisions of size A and B but not C. How can we cater for that – and how can a role specification articulate it?

Unfortunately it cannot. An engagement manager running a programme board for a major project would be expected to make decisions in relation to this board; not only low-level decisions, but also perhaps the need to cancel an important meeting or to invite a new person on to the board. These are not insignificant choices – but neither are they earth shattering. But what if the engagement manager decided, on his own authority, to push back the production date of the system which the programme was steering? Immediately we would say that this was wrong; it was not his decision to take; his customers should have been consulted. There is perhaps a clue here. Might we not argue that an individual should have the authority to make decisions over those things for which they have 'ownership'? This would certainly satisfy the engagement-manager example quoted above. More than that, taking such a view might allow us to articulate this authority boundary in the role specification too. Thus, to our four topics identified thus far we can now add 'Financial Authority' and 'Ownership'.

6.6.3 Critical Answers for Effective IT Organizations

How these two particular questions are answered will be critical for the overall effectiveness of the IT function; indeed, the principle could be applied almost anywhere. The logic I follow is perfectly simple:

1. Individuals are put into a role or position which carries with it a responsibility to deliver something in a particular fashion and – most likely – in accordance with some pre-agreed parameters.

2. Having done so, we need to recognize that, in making the appointment, we have already invested a degree of trust in them.

3. Trust established, we must also recognize that we need to allow people to do the jobs we have given them – this must include taking full ownership for those things that are rightfully theirs, and giving them the authority to utilize the company's assets (money and resource, within prescribed limits) to enable successful delivery against their remit.

I suggest that the result of following this process will be an improved delivery record, effective resource utilization, and high morale within the IT function. Occasionally the IT manager might get his fingers burned by someone who does not have the personal discipline or acumen to execute his authority in a responsible manner; but these cases are likely to be infrequent, and the individual concerned is unlikely to be trusted quite so readily a second time. To rebut any counter to this proposal is simply to argue that, if we have taken step 1 – which we must – but are not prepared to accept steps 2 and 3 – which we should – then we have appointed the wrong person in the first place. Either that or we must question our own attitude to management and delegation (which I will cover in more detail in a moment).

Taking this approach of investment in ownership and authority also fits well within an organizational model driven by the need to demonstrate value, flexibility and improvement. It also sits well within any form of disaggregated structure. As Day and Wendler (1998) suggest, "performance becomes more transparent when strict financial reporting replaces internal managerial reporting", i.e. it becomes more readily evident where people are, or are not, succeeding. The kind of discrete budgetary control that accompanies delegation of real authority – 'you own this, are responsible for its success, and have X thousand dollars to ensure delivery' – can also enforce justification of value-add and business benefit, i.e. a programme manager is less likely to waste 'his' money/ resource on spurious activities if doing so brings little additional benefit and hence erodes his 'success margin'. Enabling and empowering those who can manage effectively within the realm of real ownership and authority can only be good for the function and business overall. If their success and growth lead towards commercially driven empire building (at either the macro- or micro-level) as opposed to the creation of power bases for their own sake, then is that not a good thing?

This fundamentally entrepreneurial trend also goes some way towards addressing a situation that is all too common: "attempting to create an organizational culture that is falsely based on aspirations not genuinely held by management, or on beliefs that are only superficially held, is unlikely to succeed" (Pearson, 1992). In these kinds of cultures where the 'hidden agenda' rules, managers talk readily of responsibility and authority but are all too often unwilling to transfer it.

6.6.4 The Delegation Mirage

It is most commonly assumed that there is a simple equation around delegation: one either delegates or abdicates responsibility. Delegation – which literally means allowing someone to act in your place – is the management style most will say they adhere to; in our case, the IT manager delegates his authority in those nominated within the organization to execute that for which he is personally responsible. Abdication is fundamentally the same – with the exception that the manager then refuses any responsibility for the practical outcome as soon as things start to go wrong.

The delegation equation is slightly more subtle, however, particularly in those instances where, having delegated responsibility for something, the manager never quite gives it up. Under these circumstances a constant involvement and meddling can render the responsibility no more than a mirage, as the individual concerned has effectively no power over that which he is supposed to own.

Day and Wendler's assertion (1998) that "internal disaggregation is much harder to get right because it is essentially a simulation" follows this kind of argument. The suggestion is that one reason an IT manager's pursuit of a relational, disaggregated organizational structure will be difficult to 'get right' is because the delegation and power sharing required to make it effective will be too much of a challenge. If any form of disaggregation model is to work, the delegation of associated authority with the responsibility is a prerequisite. What percentage, I wonder, of all 'budget holders' within a corporate commercial environment actually have very little control over the budget which is nominally theirs?

The delegation mirage can also be most prevalent in those businesses with a strong corporate centre. No matter how the divestment of responsibility is dressed up, "everyone knows that the corporate centre will always intervene in matters of moment. Performance is difficult to measure and individual accountability is weak" (Day and Wendler, 1998). In the area of authority delegation, this will lead to managers who are less committed, less willing to take risks, and with only superficial concern in terms of how they appear to be performing. When something goes wrong and a project runs 20% over budget, who is to blame? The centre blames the manager who blames the budget holder – who in turn blames the manager who lays the fault at the door of the corporate culture. If only 'they' had not interfered … .

Under such circumstances "it is impossible to employ performance-based incentives" (Day and Wendler, 1998) along the lines that I have been suggesting because ownership is always cloudy with too many people having a vested interest. Of course, some organizations will deliberately go about their authorization process in such a way as to attempt to ensure that everyone who could possibly have a say in the matter does so. This is even worse. Now the nominal budget holder has to satisfy not only his manager but also an entire tribe of others who, by default, must be further removed from the issues of the day and therefore are even less qualified to make an informed decision. That "lengthy authorization and consensus-building processes stifle initiative" (Day and Wendler, 1998) is so obvious that it hardly seems worth stating; yet how many companies fall into this particular trap of feeling they need a myriad of individual approvals before a penny can be spent?

6.7 Skills Implications

6.7.1 Driven by the Person/Role Fit

In this final section on resource management, I want to consider the issues relating to skills acquisition and training. Traditionally the need to acquire skills has been driven at the technical level; for instance, if a decision is taken to install the Peoplesoft ERP package, a whole raft of people may be submitted for training on the software. Based on the arguments followed through this book, I would demand that in addition to this technically based requirement (which will never go away) the drive for skills will also come from a) the personnel aspects of an individual and the role they are given, b) a desire to slow down the passage of organizational atrophy, and c) the need to respond to change driven by both business and systems evolution.

The need to respond to shortfalls in 'people skills' will increase as IT organizations move towards more flexible and relational customer-facing models. Engagement and outsourcing managers may, for example, need only rudimentary technical awareness to fulfil their particular responsibilities; however, they are likely to become much exposed in areas of general business knowledge and the need to enhance personal attributes. Thus courses such as the ubiquitous 'Finance for IT Managers' and 'Presentation Skills' might suit people in these roles very well. Their success will to a large degree be measured on the intangibles of their performance, and so 'softer' skills such as influencing, communication, and meeting management will be critical.

These kinds of people/role skill needs are further enhanced by the argument that businesses and customers are wanting solutions above products more than ever. As Foote et al. (2001) quite correctly point out, the "skills required are far broader and the accountability assumed far greater when success is ultimately measured by a customer's improved business performance rather than by a product's performance to specifications" – in the first instance one needs to be able to understand and articulate business performance from a non-IT perspective! Many of our SLA-type metrics will be technology-driven, however this is plainly not the case for all engagement roles. Additionally, we have recently suggested that people who are given jobs to do must also be given the appropriate level of responsibility and authority too. We would not expect a programmer to start delivering code in a new language without first training them; why should we expect people to take on responsibility and authority without first giving them the opportunity to understand exactly what they meant?

6.7.2 Driven by Organizational Atrophy

In Chapter 2 we considered the nature of organizations and in particular recognized that they will have a life cycle of their own. However perfect the structure that is implemented, as time passes it will become less and less aligned with both the shape of the overall business and the demands that are placed upon it. We must accept that this kind of atrophy is inevitable – unless we are in a constant state of flux, which brings with it other problems of course. I would challenge the assertion that we can do nothing about it in terms of lengthening the cycle duration.

Knowing that something is going to happen at least allows us to forward plan and, if we are lucky, engineer a little preventative maintenance

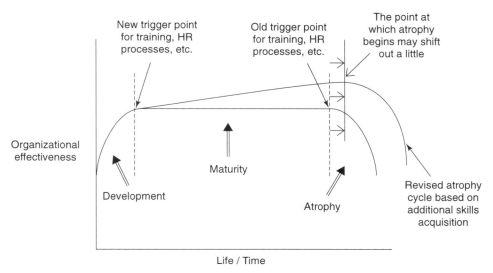

Figure 6.3. Training and the Organizational Life Cycle

along the way. Remember, we are talking about an inevitable failure of the shape and structure of the organization, not the people within it. Thus, if we have a team of six people looking after system X, over time that team may need to change to four, or ten or twenty people; maybe it will disappear altogether. Perhaps we have six development teams but over time this must rise to eight; again the end result will be a change in organizational shape, i.e. the structure we have reaches the end of its maturity cycle.

In certain cases, shrewd skills acquisition can help in prolonging the maturity cycle. Where there are increased numbers of development teams, perhaps we can begin to train additional people in readiness to take on the new roles; for the change in shape of a single team, additional training (probably largely technical) should help smooth out any formal resource transition. In Figure 6.3 we can see the effects on the atrophy model if we take a much more proactive view of skills training.

Not only do we see that the cycle may lengthen slightly, the ever-increasing portfolio of talent within the organization also suggests a slightly positive incline throughout the maturity cycle, i.e. it helps with the goal of continuous improvement. For many people, such a model is tagged with the label of a 'learning organization'; Pearson (1992) describes this as "an organization that facilitates the learning of all its members and in

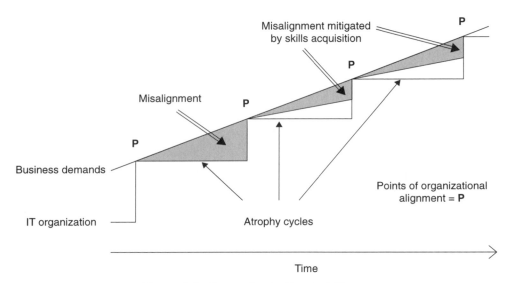

Figure 6.4. *Responding to Constant Change*

doing so continuously transforms itself". This transformation is at the level of the skills acquired and maintained within the structure of course, and not the transformation of the organization itself. Undertaking such a positive programme is undoubtedly another argument for ensuring that we have appropriate HR skills closely allied with the IT function.

6.7.3 Driven by the Constant Need for Change

As the IT organization does not exist in a vacuum, it is inevitable that there will be a gradual misalignment with the business it serves. After all, it would be some achievement for the IT manager to be able to ensure perpetual concord in an environment where, not only was his own organization in a state of flux, but also the business models he was trying to serve were evolving too. However, it is a reality that his customers' needs will change, and that this change is likely to be gradual and cumulative (perhaps imperceptibly so) rather than subject to some massive commercial jump. In Figure 6.4 I have attempted to show how business change and the IT organization may be aligned – albeit briefly! – over time.

Here we can see that at certain points – 'P' – the IT manager can be confident that he has optimized his organization to meet business demand.

However, through a cyclical process – which will, most likely, correspond to the IT atrophy model – gaps will appear between demand and capability. We can see how, with appropriate training and skills acquisition, the IT manager may be able to mitigate against the inexorable demand for change.

Enhancing overall skill-sets takes on additional dimensions in this space too. Given ever-changing demands from the business, customer-facing units need "a broad range of talent" (Foote et al., 2001) which is flexible – and this flexibility is one thing that challenges structure. If we assume that we can never have a perfectly flexible organization capable of responding to every customer demand, then perhaps, by instilling additional flexibility in our people, we can compensate to some degree. This implies broadening the skill base at the level of the individual.

It also offers some very positive opportunities for people too. If, for example, demand from the business can only be satisfied by increasing the number of projects undertaken – and therefore increasing the number of people in IT with the skills needed to run those projects – we may reach the kind of situation envisaged by Pearson (1992) with "project teams, their composition, building and development and their flexible/rotating leadership by expertise, provide an exciting vehicle for leadership training and experience". Note that I am referring to increasing the pool of skills, not increasing the number of people. The IT manager will need to adopt this approach when he is working in an environment where taking on additional resources is impossible.

6.7.4 And in the 'Static' Parts of the Organization?

In case anyone is under the misconception that business change – and the need to respond to it – will only have an effect on the front-end units, we need to correct that here. The operations area, for example, whilst regarded by many as comprising of relatively 'static' reactive units, will still be subject to the same kind of organizational atrophy as elsewhere in the IT function. The kinds of change it must respond to may be different, but they will still exist:

- Software changes – perhaps many of these will not appear major, but an upgrade in the version of a database management system can demand significant skills enhancement.

- Hardware changes – simply assuming that 'a server is a server' may be inaccurate, and the latest models of servers and PCs may require some form of skill acquisition, particularly if the function is also responsible for an element of hardware maintenance.

- Process changes – those major systems implementations that are delivered by the front-end units in response to customer-led business demands, may take a little time to filter through to the back-end support functions; but that new billing system will require new understanding within operations – for example, on the help desk or with the operators who support the system's overnight batch-type processing jobs.

There are other parts of the function that we may well view as 'static', i.e. not in the direct line of sight for constant business change. These too will be manned by individuals who can contribute to the overall improvement of the function through the enhancement of their own skills. The project office or programme support functions might be examples of such elements within the organization. What about the IT manager's team of direct reports, too? If their remit is primarily one of man management rather than 'hands on' delivery of systems and capability, then surely there must be an argument for ensuring the maintenance of a significant level of man-management or soft skills.

One final area that may or may not be utilized within the organization is a research and development (R&D) function. Whilst certainly not static in one sense, it would be possible to see these people as removed from the front line of business drivers, enmeshed as they would surely be in working at the leading edge of IT technology. Whilst their skills acquisition efforts will revolve primarily around new systems capabilities, it is possible to see how they need to become proficient analysts too – not just in terms of technology, but also in being able to see trends and predict future successes and failures. Wherever we see them in the structure, we should not lose sight of the fact that technology training alone may not be enough.

6.7.5 Knowledge Management

One final thought around resource matters – and skills implications in particular – arises from consideration of knowledge management. Boosting people's breadth and depth of skills is not simply a matter of sending them on formal training courses. Other methods – such as use of the in-house HR staff – are also open. One that is gaining more and more momentum is that of knowledge management (KM); the storing, organization, codifying and dissemination of relevant information. If "the learning organization … is flexible … responsive to changes in technology, customer requirements and other extraneous developments" (Pearson, 1992), then KM undoubtedly has a role to play. If a database administrator goes on a training course and returns with some form of training support in electronic media, then the simple act of posting this to a KM intranet will enable that knowledge to be shared by more people – or, at the very least, others will know who to turn to if they need that information.

More than that, from an organizational perspective a decentralized or disaggregated function will, to some extent, live or die by the communication and knowledge shared between its constituent parts. In a decentralization environment, for people like Peter F. Drucker (1909–) "high-quality information [is] the key to successful decision-making" (see Boylan, 2001). This is only logical given that in a traditional hierarchy decisions are made by specific individuals, but in any kind of matrix or relational organization there may be a number of people who are required to agree – and therefore they must make their decision from a consistent information base as far as this is possible. Such an argument is also supported by Day and Wendler (1998) for whom "the need to manage knowledge more effectively is both a primary driver of disaggregation and a practical constraint on it … [it] helps to solve the knowledge challenge by increasing a corporation's 'surface area', or the number of points at which it has access to knowledge".

In many respects knowledge management and skills transference are synonymous. Given a move towards an organizational model that demonstrates many aspects of disaggregation, the IT manager could find himself with a structure comprising of many relatively small teams. This is far from a barrier to information transference as "knowledge generation [skills transfer] also functions better in smaller units because the greater autonomy that comes with smaller scale is a strong complement with knowledge-generating activities" (Day and Wendler, 1998).

Conclusion

7

7.1 Summary of Considerations

For many it may seem unfortunate that, at the end of this study, there is no magic template or algorithm to be unveiled which, if applied, will guarantee the perfect IT organization to match any circumstance. We could take two virtually identical enterprises with the same geographic locations, size, turnover, outlet configuration and so forth, and be certain that when it came to IT provision differences would be inevitable. These might not be major differences either: perhaps one runs two corporate databases compared with the other's three; perhaps one chooses to outsource its help desk facility. Whatever the variations might be, there would surely be an impact on our ideal IT organization. Of course, even if the impossible did occur and they were truly the same, then one could be sure that at the corporate level culture and approach would create divergence.

Under these conditions, I feel that the most appropriate way to conclude this study is firstly with a review of some of the major topics and issues that we have discussed. Rather than simply summarize all that has gone before, I have taken the option of including a checklist of questions which, were you just about to start your reorganization, would prove a useful jumping-off point. It is almost certain that you will not know the answers to all of them – but simply lifting the lid on some of these issues will help you advance a step closer to your final goal.

Organizational Objectives

- Is there a clear understanding of the objectives and goals of the IT function in the following areas:
  - Vision – Do you have a vision for the organization?

- o Leadership – Is your leadership established, its style clear and accepted?

- o Efficiency – Do you know how effective the department is, and are there goals defined in terms of what needs to be achieved?

- o Process – How process-bound is the function? Is there an absence or over-abundance of procedures? Is it clear what will be needed when going forwards?

- o Alignment – How is the function currently aligned with its customers both inside and outside the enterprise? Is this alignment clear and positively supported by the business? Is it appropriate? Do you know where the problem areas lie?

- Moving forwards, do you have a model in terms of how the function should approach the following:

- o Planning – At what level do you intend to plan the organization's workload, deliverables, budgets, etc.? How much granularity is needed within plans? Who will be responsible for co-ordinating your planning activity? Will you adopt planning standards across the function?

- o Administration (organization) – How do you intent to maintain processes and procedures that relate to the running and organization of the function? How much local control/freedom will be given to the various subsets within the function?

- o Command – What will be your command model? How much of your authority will be delegated and to whom? What will be your model for escalation throughout the department?

- o Co-ordinate – What model do you envisage putting in place to ensure cohesive cross-functional co-ordination? How will you handle your management team?

- o Control – How do you need to report upwards and outwards in terms of the function's performance? What do you want to know in terms of regular reporting to you? Are you going to instigate standard reporting across all subfunctions?

Having answered the questions above, cross-check the two sets of answers. Are there any obvious areas of conflict between the goals you are setting and the models you tend to put in place to achieve them? (For example, allowing complete freedom to act within subsets of the function, but demanding consistent processes and reporting from all.) If so, resolve these conflicts now by adjusting your goals and models.

Strategic Value and Operational Importance

- In terms of the IT estate, do you have a clear and comparative under-standing of the elements for which you are responsible in terms of:
  - business applications (such as SAP or a payroll system)?
  - technical infrastructure (such as e-mail or a data storage platform)?
  - internal functions (such as capacity planning or the help desk)?
- Is this judgement of strategic value and operational importance seen from the perspectives of both the function's customers and the function itself?

After undertaking this analysis you should be able to clearly articulate those elements of your empire which are critical to either the business and/or the IT function, and those which may be making the least contribution. (For reference, see Figure 1.1.)

Organizational Shape

- Do you have a clear view as to the nature of the current organizational structure, i.e. is it hierarchical, flat, matrix/relational or multi-skilled?
- If it varies by subfunction, can you identify these variations?
- Can you see any obvious instances of where the current structural shape is failing?
- In terms of the overall business within which the IT organization sits, is it possible to make the same judgement at the corporate level?

Once you have answered these questions, you should be able to make an assessment of the current organizational shape and take a view as to its suitability a) within the present IT environment, b) with the present IT resource, and c) within the context of the business overall. Try to overlay some of these findings with any failings or weaknesses identified in your organizational, strategic and operational importance analyses. This should give you a valuable pointer towards the future.

Management Style

- Take a look at your management style (or perhaps undertake a 360-degree feedback exercise) and identify the kind of manager you are: Zeus, Apollo, Athena or Dionysus.

197

- Do the same for the current management team.

- How is management authority established within the function/business? Is it relational, traditional or charismatic?

- Is there a prevalent management style/authority throughout the rest of the company, and if so, what is it?

- Based on the organizational objectives you have drafted, what kind of management style is likely to be needed? Also, what kind of management approach may be required: interpersonal, informational or decisional? Also answer these questions for any specific areas of the IT organization (e.g. operations) if you are in a position to do so.

- Cross-check current management styles and approaches against what will be needed in the future.

Having gone through this exercise you should be able to identify where your management challenges lie in terms of style and approach. If you are setting clear objectives which require a management regime that is simply not natural to you, then you will need to consider a) making some changes to the objectives to fit the way you work, or b) changing your own approach. (The latter is very difficult!) You should also identify any similar misalignments within your management team. This will be food for thought when it comes to allocating management roles in the new structure. (For reference, see Table 2.3.)

Culture

- Can you define the overriding culture of the function based on the four components of: management style, management approach, leadership quality and organizational shape?

- Are there any weaknesses in or conflicts between these four?

- When people talk of 'culture', are you aware of the issues focusing on any of these components?

- Does the enterprise have an overriding culture and, if so, can you articulate it in terms of the four elements above?

You need to establish an appreciation of the present culture – and where it may be 'flawed' – and the overall company culture within which it fits. If this proves difficult, I suggest undertaking a very simple staff survey within the IT organization to attempt to root out any underlying issues. You will need to establish a positive culture to help the new organization move forwards; assuming that the present one will suffice could be fatal.

Structural Building Blocks

- Can you break down the current IT organization into a small number of fundamental component parts?

- Do they follow the model of Operations – Help Desk – Development – Engagement – Project Management (or Operations – Development – 'Services')?

- If not, can they be adapted to fit, or are there other fundamental units that must be recognized?

The objective here is to begin to gain an understanding of not only the current organizational shape, but also the major building blocks – that first layer of structure – that you will need to put in place when moving forwards. There can be some significant challenges awaiting here. Your present structure may have eight or ten large elements each with an overall manager, and together this group would probably comprise your management team. If it is likely that you will identify the need for only three or four major components in the new organization, do not shirk the challenges associated with the changes implied; and certainly do not base a new structure on the numbers of senior managers currently in post.

Customer Engagement

- Identify how IT's customers are presently engaged. Are there variations between areas, either business or IT?

- Are some relationships clearly functioning better than others? If so, why?

- How committed does the business appear in terms of its engagement with IT? Again, are there variations here, and if so, what are these and why do they occur?

- Is there a standard engagement process, e.g. in areas such as business case production or work-stack prioritization? If so, how well is this working, and where are the problems?

- Examine the programme/project initiation process. Is this blatantly tailored towards the needs of the IT community, or does it work well for the business too? (If you are not sure, ask them.)

Here we are trying to establish how effective the engagement process is. If there are procedures – and people – that are working well, then these should be the things upon which you build when moving forwards. Identification of how committed your customers are to the way you currently engage them is perhaps the most critical. Whatever you put in place in the new organization must work for both communities.

Customer Alignment

- How is IT aligned to the business at present, i.e. is it by business unit, customer, or product grouping? If this is unclear, on what basis has the current alignment been established? It could be 'political', for example.

- Are these alignment relationships formally managed or do they progress more or less haphazardly?

- Is there is an area of the business community that is the commercial driver behind the organization? This is likely to be either sales/customer or product.

- Are there areas of the business that have only peripheral formal contact with the IT function? Typically this will be in areas such as marketing and human resources.

If you are to ensure adoption of the most appropriate alignment model when moving forwards, then you not only need to understand how the present one functions but also take yourself outside of IT to gain a global perspective. Effectively this means answering the question 'what is the most important area of the business?' Identifying peripheral contacts is important too. Such alignment may be a perfectly valid model in some cases; in others, the IT function may well be missing commercially positive opportunities.

Supplier Engagement and Alignment

- Identify how IT's suppliers are presently engaged. Are there variations between them?

- Are some relationships clearly functioning better than others? If so, why?

- How committed do suppliers appear in terms of their engagement with IT? Again, are there variations here, and if so, what are these and why do they occur?

- Is there a standard supplier management process? If so, how well is this working, and where are the problems?

200

- Are supplier relationships formally managed or do they progress more or less haphazardly?

- Are there any suppliers who have only peripheral formal contact with the IT function?

Arguments for undertaking this kind of analysis are similar to that for the customer. In this area, however, findings will be obviously relevant for a) consideration of outsourcing arrangements, and b) potential commercial cost-saving opportunities through more effective engagement.

Resource Pools

- Are there any resource pools currently utilized within the IT function? If so, what are they and do they work?

- Does the business make use of such organizational structures elsewhere, or is it something that is perhaps not encouraged as a matter of HR policy?

- Can you identify potential functions within IT that could be resourced from dedicated pools of resource? (One way to answer this question is to look for the same job title – e.g. 'project manager' – repeated in different functional areas within the current structure.)

It makes sense to establish possible pooling opportunities as early as possible as this can have a major influence on your final structure. Do not attempt to 'force' resource pools into existence – but on the other hand, do not assume that they simply do not exist, or that your particular organization is so 'complex' as to warrant them unworkable.

Portfolio Management

- Do you *really* understand the totality of your function?

The message here is quite simple: if you are starting from a low knowledge/information base, then undertake a portfolio management exercise. It will prove as important as building proper foundations for a new house. There are too many benefits to be gained from this formal exercise to exclude it. Not only will these help you define your new structure – and answer many of the questions above – but also provide longer-term benefits from the perspective of putting together and maintaining IT strategies and budgets. This is the one area where I would perhaps suggest that some external specialist management consultancy might prove worthwhile.

Understanding Your People

- Is there any form of resource profiling in place for IT staff? If so, what is it, is it being used, and does it work?

- Is there a performance appraisal process that is actively followed and utilized? This might manifest itself best in the development and execution of training and development plans.

- How do the staff within IT feel about the way they are managed as people within both the function in particular, and the business as a whole? Do they care?

- Are there succession plans and/or key resource lists that are current and maintained?

- Do you have a view of the high-flyers and ambitious staff within the function?

- Can you identify those who are falling short?

- How does the relationship with HR function at present? Does it follow any kind of formal process?

- Canvass your managers; is the IT–HR relationship working? If not, where does it fall down?

An exercise such as this, undertaken at this stage, is not really about making judgements on individuals. Rather it is there to establish whether or not there are the mechanisms in place which will allow you, as IT manager, to know – and therefore get the best out of – those who work for you. Establishing the status of the HR relationship is critical too. Earlier in the book I have advocated that there should be an HR professional working full-time within the IT organization (if warranted by size, etc.). Having said that, it may be that your organization enjoys a fantastic relationship with its colleagues in HR such that nothing needs to be changed. Recognize whether this is the case or not; never make assumptions.

Reward and Recognition

- Establish whether or not the present rewards process is perceived to be working for those in IT. Is there, for example, general depression around pay-review time every year? Would this be due to the process rather than the size of the awards?

- Is there a bonus mechanism in place, and if so, is it working?

- Do you have any flexibility for implementing modified or additional bonus processes within the IT function? If so, are there any limits or caveats attached to these?

You need to establish how much room for manoeuvre you have in terms of paying people. In the vast majority of cases, I suspect that you will be governed by corporate policy that provides little flexibility for local variation. You need to know this now in order to give you time to plan and agree any changes so that you can announce these along with the new structure. Doing so will help give the impression of a fully thought-through organization.

Job Descriptions

- What is the current status of job descriptions within the IT function? Do they exist? Do they follow a standard template? If they exist, are they used?

- Are people aware of their roles in terms of deliverables, measurables, activities, attitude, responsibility and accountability?

Just getting answers to these two items will give you all you need to know with respect to job descriptions. Unless you are particularly lucky, the answers will be that job descriptions are there, but that they are variable in quality, more or less follow a standard template, but are never really used. Additionally, virtually everyone will be unable to articulate their role based on the six elements suggested. Having established this, one of the keys for you will be to decide exactly how far to go with job descriptions. If you are putting in place an entirely new organizational structure, then you should have job descriptions for every job; this means that if you go for something reasonably comprehensive here (all six elements, for example), then there will be a significant initial overhead. Having said that, most likely you will be appointing people into new roles – and they should want to know exactly what is expected of them. For this aspect alone, job descriptions can prove a good sanity check. So, a bit like portfolio management, a significant undertaking, but one that you may just have to take on – and be committed to subsequently. Starting with a flourish and then letting the process fall by the wayside may cast a shadow over your management abilities.

7.2 Some Final Thoughts

Without question, undertaking something as complex as the reshaping of an IT organization offers managers more chances to go astray than it does to succeed. Indeed, there would be those who might forcefully assert it is the kind of puzzle that is impossible to complete. I think we have seen enough throughout our discussions to suggest that the shaping of an organization – and particularly an IT organization – is never going to be one of those things under which you can draw a line and then slip to the back of a metaphorical cupboard somewhere.

Because of this – and because of the need to be able to respond to its inevitable dynamics – the IT manager needs also to ensure that he does not build management failure into the organization he launches. The comment with regard the maintenance of job descriptions, above, is a perfect example of this. Much like defining IT strategies, outlining new and impressive IT organizations is an opportunity for its architect to demonstrate the depth to which he knows just how things should be done. The danger here is that he finds himself unwittingly committing to a vast array of perfectly valid management processes and tools which, when combined, actually create an administrative monster that is impossible to execute.

In addition to job descriptions, other areas of quicksand tend to lie disguised around performance and resource management processes, commitments to the business in terms of engagement procedures, and reporting. It is all too easy to promise, over-stretch, and then fail to deliver. In certain circumstances such failure may not actually matter that much in practical terms, but this also implies broken promises to staff, customers or executives. As soon as you break a promise, you take a hit on your credibility; why should you be believed quite so readily next time? So the simple message is that you should commit only to that which is achievable. Indeed, I can point to a number of relevant 'commandments' from an earlier work: "Only promise what you know you can deliver; failure to deliver even small things can erode confidence; nothing should be unmanaged" (Gouge, 2001).

As you take your journey through the process that is organizational reshaping, you will, of course, make many mistakes. Never be put off by this inevitability – and never use it as a reason for doing nothing. Along the way there will be things you try that will prove huge successes, and others that will become embarrassing white elephants. One of the key things is to try. If you think you can define a smart new way of drawing up your organization chart, then try it. If you have an idea for managing resource pools, sanity check the notion with some people you trust and then see if it works. Be prepared to experiment a little – and be prepared for those who work with you to experiment a little too. Above all else, believe in what you are doing and be committed to its success. After all, if these are attributes that you do not demonstrate, why should anyone else?

References

A – Journals and Articles

Barton N. (2002) Business Innovation Through IT *Compass* www.cmp-com.newcomweb.demon.com/home_whitepapers.htm *Accessed August 2002*

Beck J. (2002) IT Services Sourcing Goes Strategic *Gartner 'Article Top View' AV-16-2109* www4.gartner.com/resources/106000/106031/106031.pdf *Accessed August 2002*

Bell M. (2002) The Five Principles of Organisational Resilience *Gartner 'Article Top View' AV-15* 0508 www4.gartner.com/resources/103600/103658/103658.pdf *Accessed July 2002*

Boylan P. (2001) Introduction to the Theoretical and Philosophical basis of Modern Management *Lecture Notes* www.web.city.ac.uk/art-spol/theorymgt.html *Accessed August 2002*

Brittain K. and Matlus R. (2002) Road Map for IT Service-Level Management *Gartner 'Article Top View' AV-15-2307* www4.gartner.com/resources/104100/104108/104108.pdf *Accessed July 2002*

Cimral J., Lawler M. and Crowley T. (2002) Getting Started with Portfolio Management *Pro Sight Inc.* www.prosight.com/downloads/ProSightPBIA_200207.pdf *Accessed August 2002*

Da Rold C. (2001) Sourcing Strategy: Evaluate Your Ability Before Moving *Gartner 'Research Note' DF-14-2418* www4.gartner.com *Accessed July 2002*

Da Rold C. (2002) Sourcing Strategy: Evaluate the Six Alternatives *Gartner 'Research Note' DF-15-4908* www4.gartner.com *Accessed July 2002*

Day J. (2001) Organising for Growth *McKinsey Quarterly 2001* www.mckinseyquarterly.com/ar_g.asp?ar=1029 *Accessed July 2002*

Day J. and Wendler J. (1998) The New Economics of Organization *McKinsey Quarterly 1998* www.mckinseyquarterly.com/ar_g.asp?ar=275 *Accessed August 2002*

Diromualdo A. (1998) Strategic Intent for IT Outsourcing *Sloan Management Review* www.smr.mit.edu/past/1998/smr3945.html *Accessed August 2002*

Dreyfuss C. (2002) Aligning Services with Business Objectives by Sourcing *Gartner 'Research Note' COM-15-8326* www4.gartner.com *Accessed July 2002*

Eisenstat R., Foote N., Galbraith J., and Miller D. (2001) Beyond the business unit *McKinsey Quarterly 2001* www.mckinseyquarterly.com/ar_g.asp?ar=989 *Accessed July 2002*

Foote N., Galbraith J., Hope Q. and Miller D. (2001) Making solutions the answer *McKinsey Quarterly 2001* www.mckinseyquarterly.com/ar_g.asp?ar=1080 *Accessed July 2002*

Mahoney J. (2001) Even Change is Changing: Now its Organizational Angst *Gartner 'Article Top View' AV-14-0470* www4.gartner.com/resources/99800/99818/99818.pdf *Accessed July 2002*

Meta Group, The (2002) The Business of IT Portfolio Management: Balancing Risk, Innovation, and ROI *The Meta Group* www.meta-group.com/cgi-bin/inetcgi/jsp/displayarticle.do?oid=32945 *Accessed August 2002*

Sturges D. and Brewerton F. (2002) Organizational Engineering: A New, Old Way to View Organisations and their Management *University of Texas-Pan American* www.baclass.panam.edu/course/intb436/reliability.htm *Accessed August 2002*

B – Books

Gouge I., *On the 7th Day – Strategy and planning for successful IT projects*, Management Books 2000, Chalford (2001)

Nyström H., 'Organizational Innovation' in *Innovation and Creativity at Work*, West M. and Farr J. (eds), John Wiley, Chichester (1996)

Pearson G., *The Competitive Organisation*, McGraw-Hill, London (1992)

Ward J., Griffiths P. and Whitmore P., *Strategic Planning for Information Systems*, John Wiley, Chichester (1990)

Index